Miller Barber
Orville Moody
Bob Rosburg
Dave Marr
Doug Sanders
Tommy Aaron
and Lou Graham

Illustrations by Dom Lupo

TOP TIPS from SENIOR PROS

with Desmond Tolhurst

SIMON AND SCHUSTER

New York   London   Toronto   Sydney   Tokyo   Singapore

Acknowledgments

No book worth reading comes together without the best efforts and talents of many people. We are very grateful to all those who brought *Top Tips from Senior Pros* to the bookstores, but especially want to thank Leonard Kamsler for his fine action photos on which artist Dom Lupo based his illustrations, and writer Desmond Tolhurst, who did such an excellent job of putting our ideas on paper. Our thanks also go to Bev Norwood of IMG, who oversaw the project, and to Jeff Neuman, our editor at Simon and Schuster. It was Jeff who came up with the idea for this book, and we are delighted to be a part of it.

Simon and Schuster
Simon & Schuster Building
Rockefeller Center
1230 Avenue of the Americas
New York, New York 10020

SIMON AND SCHUSTER and colophon are registered trademarks of Simon & Schuster Inc.

Designed by Levavi & Levavi/Mary Beth Kilkelly
Manufactured in the United States of America

10 9 8 7 6 5 4 3 2 1

Library of Congress Cataloging in Publication Data
Top tips from senior pros/Miller Barber . . . [et al.] with Desmond Tolhurst; illustrations by Don Lupo.
    p. cm.
    1. Golf. I. Barber, Miller, date. II. Tolhurst, Desmond.
GV965.T64   1990
796.352'3–dc20   89-49663
                                                          CIP

ISBN 0-671-68445-0

Contents

MILLER BARBER   7

Keep the right posture·Square is straight·Use your head·A "risky" wood made safe·Tree trouble·Those awkward lies·Explode with ease·Warm up your short game·Putting: an arm-and-shoulder model

ORVILLE MOODY   29

Cure the "reverse"·Square your takeaway·When you need to hook out of trouble·Fading out of trouble·The high shot·The low shot· Into the wind·Downwind·Try a long putter for a smooth stroke

BOB ROSBURG   51

Time to change your grip?·Watch your back!·Vary your address· When the ball is below·When the ball is above·Play it smart from rough·Downhill at the back·Make your pitches count·Give my putting style a try

DAVE MARR   73

Everyman's warmup·Cure for a fast backswing·The feet-together drill·Stopping the sway·The long explosion shot·Uphill in the front·Blocked backswing·Accelerate through on the green, too·Spot your putts

DOUG SANDERS   95

Beat the "freezes"·Tuck the right arm in·Swing a heavy club·Make the wind your friend·Ball above in the bunker·The divot-hole shot· Water? Just skip it!·The 3-wood chip·The Texas Wedge

TOMMY AARON   117

The baseball drill·Light is right·Watch your ball position·Fairway bunkers—catch it cleanly·Downhill lies·Uphill lies·Irons from the rough: short, steep, and open·The soft lob·The equator shot

LOU GRAHAM   139

Get the right hold·Seniors, it's time for a change of address·To lengthen your backswing, think *hips*·Dig it out·A tough lie·Let 'em laugh: putt from the sand·Up and out of the water·Explode from deep rough·Chipping made simple

Introduction

Over the years, innumerable swing theories and hard-to-understand treatises on the game of golf have been published in book or article form. These have tended to overwhelm readers looking not to remake their whole game, but to improve on what they've spent a lifetime doing. We decided to take an entirely different tack here. Although nothing can take the place of a series of live lessons, every one of the lessons in this book, as much as possible, resembles a session with your PGA professional. It addresses one subject and one subject only, and the instruction is short, precise, and crystal clear.

There are 63 lessons in all, covering every aspect of the game. We have included the fundamentals of golf, from a sound grip and stance to developing a fine swing, one that will give you power as well as accuracy. We also have supplied tips on shotmaking, correcting faults, trouble shots, bunker play, the short game, and putting. Whatever your problem, you can take the solution we recommend straight to the practice ground or the course.

Best of all, the lessons have worked well for us in competition. They're not just opinions. They've been tournament tested—on the regular Tour as well as the Senior Tour.

MILLER BARBER

MILLER BARBER

Born in Shreveport, Louisiana, in 1931, Miller Barber took to golf as a high school sophomore. At the University of Arkansas, he won the Southwest Conference Championship in 1951. He had a three-year hitch in the Air Force starting in 1956, and won the Air Force Championship in 1957. Turning pro in 1959, Barber didn't win his first Tour event until 1964, but from 1967 to 1974 he won at least one event a year, a record equaled only by Jack Nicklaus. He had a career total of eleven Tour victories. He was a member of the 1969 and 1971 Ryder Cup Teams. On the Senior Tour, which he joined in 1981, he has been nothing less than sensational, with twenty-four victories through the end of 1988, an average of three wins a year. These victories include the 1981 PGA Seniors, 1982, 1984, and 1985 U.S. Senior Opens, and the 1983 Senior TPC. Although Barber has an unusual backswing, closing the clubface while taking the club up steeply with a flying right elbow, his excellent rhythm and timing enable him to come through the ball in copybook fashion. He is one of the longest, and certainly one of the straightest drivers on the Senior Tour, and has great touch around the greens. He is a marvelous putter.

Keep the Right Posture

Probably one of the most overlooked aspects of address is correct posture. It may not be an exciting topic, but if you get it right, your body is at least set to make a powerful swing. If you get it wrong, you can never develop much power or build a sound, grooved swing.

The majority of the seniors I see who have poor posture (smaller illustration) invariably reach for the ball, their hands too far away from their body, leaning too far forward. To balance themselves, they usually tend to stiffen their legs. I think the root cause of reaching for the ball is that it feels powerful. In fact, it's not. Because your head is so far forward you tend to see the swing as a "straight line" action, and take the club straight back from the ball along the target line, and through along the target line. Instead of turning your shoulders correctly going back, you lift your right shoulder and drop your left shoulder in a rocking motion. On the forward swing, your shoulders again work in too vertical a plane and your hips tend to slide to the left and lock. You block the release, meaning the arms cannot square the clubface at impact. Often, the clubface remains open and you slice. Occasionally, your hands will snap the clubhead closed and you hit a duck hook.

The larger illustration shows the points you should work on: The chin is up, giving clearance for the shoulder turn; the back is straight and tilted forward just slightly from the hips; the club is a comfortable distance away from the

body; the arms are hanging down from the shoulders, and the knees are slightly flexed. This correct posture allows you to turn your shoulders away from the ball in the backswing on a correct, flatter plane, taking the club back to the inside as your hands and arms swing the club up. On the forward swing, your hips can shift to the left and then turn to the left out of the way, giving room for your hands and arms to swing the club through the ball freely. You then can release the club correctly, squaring the clubface with the ball by impact, hitting it solidly and straight.

Square Is Straight

The address position is much like aiming a gun. If you don't have the target in your sights, you're not going to hit the bull's-eye. If you're on target, it's merely a matter of pulling the trigger. If you're not hitting the ball straight, the first thing you should check is your address, and the first thing to check at address is your "aim," or body alignment. Your alignment plays such a large part in setting up the path on which you swing the club, and thus the direction of your shots.

For most golfers a square alignment is best for full shots, with imaginary lines across the toes, hips, and shoulders (called the foot, hip, and shoulder lines) parallel or square to your target line, the line from your ball to the target. This is because, as a general rule, if your foot line is square, it's more likely that the hip and shoulder lines will be square, too. However, of the three lines, it is the shoulder line that is critical, as it sets up the swing path. If your shoulders are set left of parallel, then you're likely to swing outside in and pull the ball left. If they're set right of parallel, you'll tend to swing inside out and push the ball right. If the clubface meanwhile is aimed at the target, then at impact it probably will be open or closed respectively to these swing paths, and you'll also slice and hook the ball.

If you're not hitting the ball straight, you should first check your alignment with the aid of a friend. Set up to the ball, aiming at a definite target. Then have your friend lay down a club just outside your intended line of swing, and another across your toes. This probably will indicate a body alignment to the left or right of parallel to the target line. Then rearrange the clubs as shown in the illustration, placing the club just outside the target line parallel to the line, and the club across the toes parallel to the first club. Now hit some balls. If you're still not hitting straight, then it could be that your foot line is parallel, but your hip and shoulder lines are not. Take your address again, and then check by picking up the club and laying it first across the shoulders and then across the hips as shown.

When you're satisfied that your foot, hip, and shoulder lines are all parallel to the target line, continue to hit. Once the square alignment again feels comfortable, you should soon start to hit the ball straight.

Use Your Head

It's a fact that the majority of seniors—and I play with dozens each year—could lower their handicaps by up to half a dozen strokes merely by planning ahead out on the course. As a working example, look at the illustration, which shows a hole of around 350 yards. The bunkers in the landing area for the tee shot are out 200 to 220 yards.

Because of the length of the hole, many players, I'm sure, would simply take out their drivers and fire away. That's not good strategy, because you're ignoring the fairway bunkers placed right in the area where your normal drive will land. All you have to do is miscue the shot a little, and you'll land up in one of the bunkers (B). If you think for a moment, you can see that an easy 3- or 4-wood from the tee would place you in the fairway 190 yards out, and well short of the bunkers (A). You even can miss the shot a little and it won't hurt—you'd still only have around 160 yards into the green below, a 5-iron shot for most.

On the second shot, many players probably would fire right at the flag. Now that's fine if you only have a short iron into the green and the consequences for missing the shot aren't too severe. However, here a mis-hit middle iron will go right into the water (C), a one-stroke penalty, and then you'll have a short pitch over water to the flag—not your favorite shot, I'm sure!

If you look over the situation more carefully, you can see that aiming for the left side of the green (D) is a much safer shot. If you are short, you'll have a chip and putt for par; if long or left, a chip or at worst a bunker shot, but at least you'll be dry. If you push or fade the shot, or if a fade is your natural shot, you'll be right up by the pin. Only if you go right and short will you be wet!

Examine every hole on your course in this way. Make up a game plan and stick to it as much as possible. You've nothing to lose except some unwanted strokes from your score!

MILLER BARBER

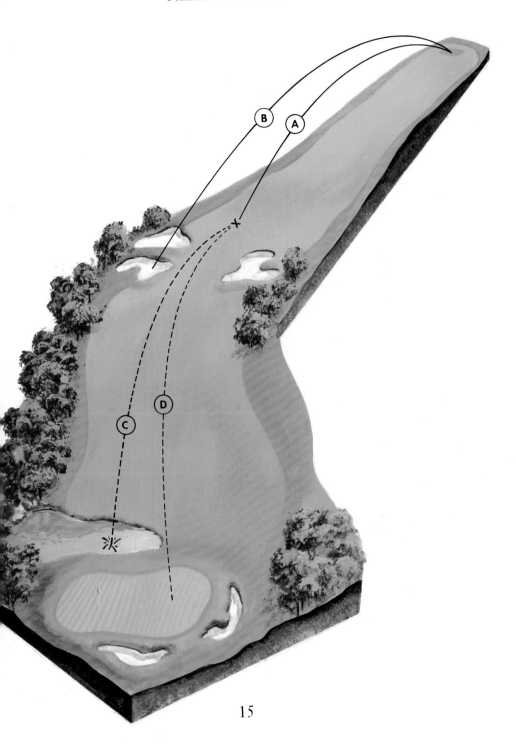

15

A "Risky" Wood Made Safe

When your drive on a par 5 or extra-long par 4 goes into the rough, you obviously want to hit for distance on your second shot. If the ball is sitting up in the rough, of course

16

there's no problem—you can take a wood and go with your normal swing. But what if the ball is lying down a bit—not so badly that you're forced to use a medium or short iron, but not so well that you don't have a tiny bit of doubt in the back of your mind? That's when it pays to know a couple of adjustments that can turn a risky shot into a safe one.

You can't go with a normal "sweeping" type of wood swing from such a lie. You'll have to force the clubhead through too much grass to get to the ball. In effect, what you want to do is make an "iron swing" with your wood; you want to take the wood up higher than usual, and then beat down more steeply on the ball.

First, in order to catch the ball cleaner, play it back a little in your stance and position your hands slightly ahead of it. This sets up a steeper takeaway with a quicker wrist break than normal so that you can hit with more of a descending blow. The second adjustment allows you to swing on a more upright plane (see illustration), further steepening the hit. This might appear difficult but really isn't. Just play the ball slightly closer to you, standing a trifle more erect than usual. Then, in the backswing, concentrate on swinging the hands and club up and down more steeply than usual.

When it comes to getting some distance from rough, you can use a wood on the better lies, or a middle iron or short iron on worse lies, but you should *never* use a long iron unless you have a perfect lie. Even on a so-so lie, a wood used with the technique described above will part and slide through the grass, putting a solid hit on the ball, but a long iron will get snagged in the grass.

Tree Trouble

One of the trickier situations is when your ball is so close to a tree or other obstacle that you can't take a normal right-handed swing. There are several ways to extricate yourself. Pick the one that suits the particular situation and your talents.

Probably the easiest method for most seniors is to stand with your back to the target, your feet slightly apart, and position the ball a little to the right of your right foot. Using a wedge, aim the leading edge at the target and grip it with the right hand only at the bottom of the handle. If you've never played or practiced the shot before, then simply punch the ball backward, using a firm wrist. This is also good if you only have a short distance to your target. However, if you practice the shot, you'll find that you can add some wrist, as I am doing in the illustration, and really get a lot of distance. In winning the final of the 1981 World Match Play at Wentworth, England, Seve Ballesteros hit a shot with a 3-iron *160 yards* in this fashion.

If you have the talent to hit a left-handed shot, turn the clubhead of a wedge upside down so that the blade faces the target and take a left-handed swing. When you hit left-handed, remember to reverse all the usual fundamentals—grip with the left hand below the right, set up with your right arm extended, your left arm bent, and so on. This is one shot you must practice before you try it on the course.

Sometimes your ball comes to rest so close to the side of a greenside bunker that to play the shot right-handed you'd be forced to stand in the bunker with the ball very much above you. Playing the shot in any other way is infinitely easier. Besides the right-hand-only shot, you can use the

back of your putter to give the ball a stiff-wristed left-handed hit, provided the putter has a plain back or a generous cavity. If you don't have the right sort of putter or have to loft the ball, you also can turn a wedge upside down and again hit the ball stiff-wristed from the left side.

Those Awkward Lies

Two lies that seem to give my pro-am partners a lot of trouble are hardpan lies and perched lies. The first looks far more difficult than it is. The second looks easy, but is deceptively difficult.

When your ball lies on hardpan (illustration, lower right), the most common mistake is to try to force it up in the air. If you play the ball forward in your stance and hit up on the ball, it's invariably fatal; you'll either hit behind the ball or skull it. Another mistake is simply swinging too quickly. This generally happens, I think, because you're afraid of the shot, and when you're scared, the tendency always is to swing much too fast. I've found it's best *not* to make any adjustments. Just trust your normal swing and the loft of the club to get the ball up for you. To keep yourself from getting too quick, which usually results in the hands moving independently of the body in the take-away, concentrate on starting the swing with the arms, shoulders, hips, and club working together. A good, coordinated takeaway is a slow takeaway.

When your ball is perched high on top of the rough (illustration, lower left), the shot doesn't look hard, but it's easy to botch. You usually hit underneath the ball and pop it up in the air. There are two causes for this: addressing the ball at ground level, which will pre-program a hit underneath it; or hitting it with too much of a descending blow, which comes from playing the ball too far back in the stance, putting too much weight on the left foot, or breaking the wrists too quickly in the backswing. To guard against these problems, address the ball with the clubface level with the ball. Choke down a little on the club to help yourself do it. Use a normal ball position, and divide your weight equally between your feet. A good key is to imagine that you're swinging a driver, even though you may be using an iron or fairway wood. You will then take the club back low and strike the ball with a sweeping blow; this is exactly what you want.

Explode with Ease

In pro-ams, most of the seniors I've ever played with fear the sand shot. They can't understand why pros say that the short sand shot from a good lie is one of the easiest shots in the game. Well, I'll let you in on a little secret. This shot really is easy, provided—and this is the key— you use the right technique.

On a short bunker shot, you need to get the ball up fairly quickly so that it clears the lip of the bunker. To do that, you need an abrupt "up and down" swing, with the wrists breaking very quickly on the backswing, taking the club up, and then a steep descent down and through the ball. It's the same principle as bouncing a ball off a concrete floor; the steeper the angle at which the ball hits the floor, the more steeply it will rebound. To help you do that, place more weight on the left foot.

To further steepen the angle of the swing, you essentially play a cut shot. In other words, open your stance and shoulders as though you were going to play a shot to the left of the target. This makes you swing back and up out- side the line, then down and through from out to in. To help you break your wrists quickly, place your right hand more on top of the grip. Play the ball a couple of inches inside your left heel. To compensate for the open body alignment, open the blade a corresponding amount (see smaller illustration). If you aim your swing path, say, five feet left of the flag, aim the leading edge of the sand wedge five feet right of the flag before taking your grip. Now go ahead and swing, planning to enter the sand about two inches behind the ball. You'll find that the club strikes the sand and then skids through, taking a shallow cut. The reason is that by opening the clubface, you've lowered the

back of the flange on the sand wedge. It can't dig, because the back of the flange, rather than the leading edge, strikes the sand first.

A little experimentation and practice will enable you to develop feel with the shot. When you're close to the hole, open the stance and blade a lot. When you're farther out, open them less. Also, on short shots take a shorter swing than on longer shots. Soon, you won't just be getting the ball out, you'll be trying to hole it and getting your share of "ups and downs," just like the pros.

Warm Up Your Short Game

Most seniors, I think, have the wrong priorities when they warm up before a game. They spend almost all of their time on the practice ground, hitting full shots, then head for the practice green. There they try a few long putts, a few short putts, and every time they miss, they just rake over another ball. They never really warm up their short game, and it is the short game that can bail you out on

those first few holes, where most strokes are lost.

A far better plan would be to spend more time on shots around and on the green. After hitting some full shots on the practice ground, go to the practice green with three balls. First, hit three bunker shots. To make this practice as realistic as possible, don't hit all three balls to the same pin; hit to three separate targets at varying distances. In golf, you only get one chance to make a shot, so you should warm up under game conditions. Besides, by practicing to three separate targets, you reestablish touch and feel. Then hit three pitch shots to different targets, and then three chips (see illustration). On each shot, go through the same pre-swing routine that you'd use on the course—visualize where you want to land the ball, read the green for any breaks, and so on. You must warm up your mind for golf as well as your muscles.

Follow the same plan in putting. First, try three long putts, again hitting each ball to a different hole. This helps you reestablish your touch. Then, put down the balls around one hole, say, six to eight feet away, so that each putt is quite different, and really work on holing all of them. The idea here is to simulate those tough putts that you are liable to leave yourself early in the game. Get a few of these under your belt and it really increases your confidence. As on the short game shots, go through your whole pre-stroke routine before putting each ball, just as if you were out on the course—from getting down behind the ball and reading the break to the number of "looks" at the hole you normally take when over the ball.

Give this type of pre-game warmup a try. I'm sure that you'll score better on those first few holes, and get each round off to a much faster start.

Putting:
An Arm-and-Shoulder Model

Putting is highly individual, but, if you favor an arm-and-shoulder type of stroke, there are several points you can learn from my style.

In the arm-and-shoulder style, you basically don't use any wrist action at all. It's almost exactly like the swing of a pendulum back and through, your two arms and the putter forming the pendulum. You make the stroke by swinging your arms and club back and through in one piece, with a rocking motion of the shoulders around a point at the base of your neck completing the action.

To keep wristiness out of the stroke, I use a palm grip in the left hand, with the club lying much closer to the lifeline of the left hand than it does in the normal left-hand grip. The grip in the right hand is more in the fingers. Note that both thumbs are on top of the shaft, rather than on the sides of the shaft as they would be on woods and irons. The "thumbs on top" position puts the thumbs in the best position for sensitive feel and is used by just about every good putter.

In the putting stroke, you don't need a lot of power. However, you do need maximum precision. It's most important never to let your head move sideways. To lock my head in place, I put 80 percent of my weight on my left foot and brace my right leg inward against my left leg. To make a good sweeping stroke, I play the ball slightly forward in the stance, a little off my left heel, my hands over the ball. I like to use a square stance, a line across my toes parallel to the intended line of putt. If your feet are square, you'll find it's easier to set up with the shoulders square,

too. Square shoulders are important because the shoulder
line will program the swing path, unless there's some ma-
nipulation of the club by the hands.

As I said above, you basically use no wrist action in this
style. The only exceptions would be on very long putts or
extraordinarily slow greens.

ORVILLE MOODY

ORVILLE MOODY

The son of a golf course superintendent, Orville Moody was born in 1933 in Chichasha, Oklahoma. Part Choctaw Indian, Moody can remember playing golf, as early "as I was big enough to hold a club." He won the Oklahoma state scholastic championship. Offered a football scholarship to the University of Oklahoma, he left college soon after enrolling in 1953, and enlisted in the Army. Soon his golfing talents were recognized, and he was put in charge of all army golf courses, serving Japan, Korea, Germany, and the United States. He won three Korean Opens and the 1965 All-Service Championship. In 1967, Staff Sergeant Moody decided to give up his fourteen-year army career to try the Tour. His greatest year came in 1969, when he won the U.S. Open at the Champions G. C., Houston, Texas, as well as the World Series of Golf, and teamed with Lee Trevino to win the World Cup for the United States. Joining the Senior Tour in 1984, Moody has enjoyed phenomenal success, mostly because he adopted a long putter in 1985. Acknowledged among his peers to be one of the finest swingers and shotmakers ever, Moody had been a very poor putter. With his new method, he became the best putter on the Senior Tour in 1988. He has won nine Senior events, as well as the 1986 and 1987 Australian PGA Championships.

31

Cure the "Reverse"

One of the most important components of power is a proper weight shift—to the right foot on the backswing and back to the left foot on the forward swing. However, many seniors I play with in pro-ams don't use their weight properly. They actually reverse the correct weight shift. They move the weight to the left foot going back (see ghosted part of illustration), then on the forward swing,

per Newton's third law, there is an equal and opposite reaction: They shift the weight to the right foot! This puts the low point of the swing arc behind the ball, leading to fat shots and skied drives. Worse, the weight is moving in the opposite direction to the one they want to hit in, so they lose a lot of power. If you find yourself heavy on your right foot in the finish, then your problem is this reverse weight shift.

There can be several reasons for the fault. The first of these is an incorrect setup. If you're using a long club such as a wood or long iron, too narrow a stance can place the body weight too much over the ball at address. From here, it's all too easy to shift the weight to the left foot. The correction would be to widen the stance by placing the right foot farther to the right. Another fault at address is actually placing more weight on the left foot, which would lead directly to a reverse weight shift. To correct this, divide the weight equally between your feet.

However, you can still reverse even if the address is correct. Many senior players grew up when one of the big fetishes in golf instruction was keeping the head stock-still. As you swing the club back, you're scared of shifting your weight to the right, because you might then move your head. You make such a big effort to keep your head still that you actually shift your weight to your left foot.

Now, I'm not saying you want to sway around like a palm tree! But you must shift your weight to your right foot going back. Do what I do, and let your body turn take about 75 percent of your weight to the right foot. Then, provided you keep your right leg firm, you can't sway. With all that weight on the right side at the top (see illustration), the equal and opposite reaction is to move it to the left. Then you develop maximum power.

Square Your Takeaway

One of the more common faults I see when playing with senior amateurs is that, instead of keeping the clubface square in the backswing, they close or open it. The problem comes from excessive rotation of the hands in the takeaway. The more you rotate your hands counterclockwise, the more you close the clubface (see illustration). The more you rotate them clockwise, the more you open it. These actions complicate the swing, because you have to compensate later in order to hit the ball straight. So, if all you want to do is hit a normal straight shot, they should be avoided.

Let's assume your hands rotate counterclockwise and close the clubface going back. Then, as a rule you will react by rotating them clockwise coming through, opening the clubface, and the usual result is a fade. However, if you don't realize you've closed the clubface—and this is particularly likely if you're not a low-handicap player—you could leave it closed and hook the ball. On the other hand, if your hands rotate clockwise going back, opening the clubface, generally speaking you will rotate counterclockwise and close it coming through, and the usual result is a draw. But high-handicappers are just as likely to leave the clubface open and slice.

One can conclude that the mixed results hand rotation gives you, not to mention the confusion these results can cause, makes it something you should leave to the experts. For the majority of seniors, it's best to work on keeping the clubface square going back. Then, at least you will be in good position to apply the club to the ball.

To do this, work in the takeaway on taking your arms and the club back with your shoulder turn as you let your wrists start cocking and your weight shift. If your shoul-

ders control your arms, there should not be any excess hand rotation. However, check at the point shown in the illustration, where the clubshaft reaches horizontal. If you've done it right, the face will be square, toe pointing up. But, if the clubface faces the ground, then you've rotated your hands counterclockwise (closed). If the clubface faces toward the sky, they've rotated clockwise (open). If you have a problem, work on the takeaway in slow motion until the square position becomes a habit.

When You Need to Hook Out of Trouble

When I'm stymied behind a tree and my pro-am partners see me drawing or hooking a ball around the tree onto the green, I can see that they admire the shot, but it's also obvious that they believe they could never do it themselves. Now let me talk to you guys directly. Yes, you can master the shot. What you don't realize is that, while you may not have the skills to draw or hook my way, because it's an advanced method, there also is an easy two-step method, one you can use to bail yourself out of trouble.

In order to draw or hook the ball, the face of the club must be closed (aimed to the left of) the path on which you're swinging the club at impact. The easiest way to achieve this is to set the blade closed at address, and then use your normal swing.

Step One is to set up as though you were going to hit a straight shot to an imaginary target to the right of the tree, where you want the ball to start (see illustrations). Aim the leading edge of the club at the imaginary target, and position your feet and shoulders on lines parallel to the line at that target. Step Two is to loosen your grip, aiming the leading edge at your actual target, and regrip, taking your normal grip. What you've done is close the blade in relation to your swing path. Now go ahead and make your usual swing. The ball will start at the imaginary target, but because of the closed clubface, you put right-to-left spin on the ball, and it finally will curve back to your actual target. To vary the amount of curve, vary your imaginary target. For a gentle draw, pick a target just a little to the right of the actual target. For a big hook, pick one well to the right. That's it.

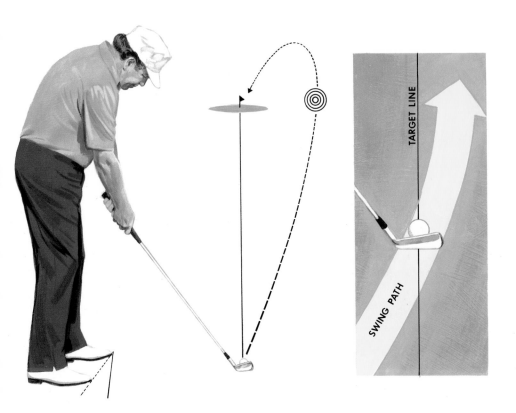

As you gain more experience, you'll probably feel the need to use a method you can fine-tune more easily. With that thought in mind, here's my method. Step One is exactly the same. Pick out the imaginary target to the right of the tree and set up as though you were going to hit straight at that target. In Step Two, I make no changes at address —I close the blade during the swing. I swing back, allowing the blade to open slightly. Then on the forward swing, I let my right hand overtake my left hand sooner in the downswing, closing the blade at impact. With this method, I can vary the curve from a three-yard draw to a big hook.

Fading Out of Trouble

You should approach the deliberate fade or slice around a tree in exactly the same way I described previously for the draw or hook. There is a simple way to play the shot, which should be used by all but low-handicap players. There's also an advanced way to play the shot, which I'll describe second. In both cases, you reverse the methods used for the draw or hook.

To fade or slice the ball, the clubface must be open (aimed to the right) of your swing path at impact. Again, the easy way to do this is simply to set the blade open at address, and then swing normally.

Step One is to set up as though you were going to hit a straight shot to an imaginary target left of the tree, on the line you wish the ball to start (see illustrations). Aim the leading edge at the imaginary target, and square your feet and shoulders to that line. Step Two is to loosen your grip, aim the leading edge at your actual target, and regrip. This sets the blade open in relation to your swing path. Now, make your normal swing and the ball will start at the imaginary target and slice back to the actual target. Again, to vary the amount of curve, vary your imaginary target. For a fade, pick a target a little left of the actual target, for a slice, pick one well to the left.

The advanced method, the one I use, has the same Step One, but the clubface is open through impact. Instead of letting the right hand roll over the left, I let it drag behind the left a little bit, leaving the face open. With this method, I find I can get much finer gradations of curve.

Whichever method you use, the hard thing about curving the ball is to swing where you're aiming—the temptation is to swing directly at the actual target. I'll give you a

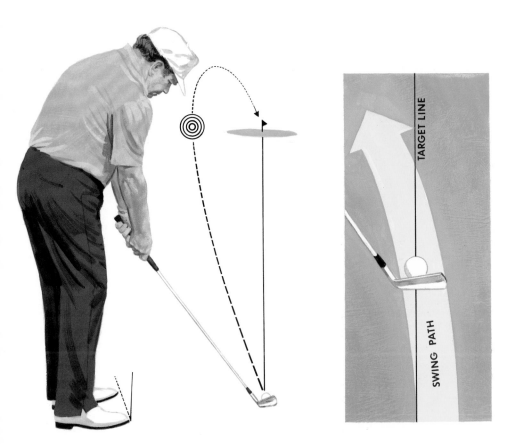

little additional aid that should do the trick. Imagine that, before setting up, you're looking straight down at the ball and that it turns into a clockface. The twelve-o'clock-to-six-o'clock axis is directly on the target line, with six o'clock on the back of the ball. If you're hitting a deliberate fade or slice, aim to hit the ball at five o'clock, and you'll swing through to the left of the actual target. The opposite is true of draws and hooks—aim to strike the ball at seven o'clock.

The High Shot

A common problem in golf is being partially stymied by a tree. Sometimes you can hook or slice around it, as described earlier. However, on other occasions the best shot is to hit the ball higher than usual, flying it over the tree to the target. Hitting up to an elevated green is another situation that calls for the high shot. The general approach to hitting a shot high is similar to that in working the ball to the left or right. There's an easy way to do it, the one I recommend to most senior amateurs. There's also a more advanced method for low-handicappers.

To hit the ball higher than usual, you must increase the effective loft of the club you're using at impact. The easiest way to do this is play the ball a few inches farther forward in your stance while leaving your hands in their normal position, about off the inside of the left thigh. Instead of the shaft leaning slightly forward as on a normal shot, the shaft would appear vertical to someone standing in front of you, and this increases the club's effective loft (see illustration). You also position more of your body weight behind the ball, another factor in driving it higher. When setting up, be certain that you square the leading edge of the club at the target before taking your grip. The tendency when playing the ball forward is to close the clubface. If you don't square it up, you'll pull the ball to the left. In the swing, the one thing you must guard against is sliding your body weight past the ball in the downswing, which would drive it low. If anything, work on staying behind the ball a little longer in the downswing as a safety measure.

In the advanced method, don't change anything at address. You're going to increase the effective loft of the club during the swing. What you do is take a normal backswing. But, at the start of the downswing, don't shift your lower body weight to the left quite as quickly as usual. At impact, you'll have more weight on the right side than normal, and you catch the ball a little on the upswing. Since the low point of the swing will be farther behind the ball than usual, you must prevent the clubface from closing too quickly, sending the ball left. So, pull through the ball strongly with your left hand.

41

The Low Shot

Sometimes your ball is under a tree or behind low over-hanging branches. If you tried to hit a shot with a normal trajectory, the ball undoubtedly would get up much too quickly and strike the tree or branches. I see many of you seniors just chip out sideways in such circumstances. That's good strategy if you really don't have a shot. How-ever, if you learn how to hit the ball low, you'll be sur-

prised how often you'll be able to advance the ball well down the fairway or even onto the green. As with other special shots I've described, there's an easy method, one I'd recommend to most seniors, even high-handicappers, and a second method that only low-handicappers should attempt.

To hit the ball lower than usual, you've got to reduce the effective loft on the club you're using at impact. The easy way to do this is to play the ball a few inches back in the stance. When you do so, remember to keep your hands in their normal position, about off the inside of the left thigh. This leans the shaft forward, hooding the club and reducing the loft. You also are positioning more of the body weight ahead of the ball, another factor in driving it lower. In the setup, be certain you square the blade at the target before taking your grip. When you play the ball back in the stance, it tends to make you open the face, and if you left it in that position, you'd push the shot to the right. Once you've made these adjustments, just go ahead and make your normal swing. With the blade pre-set with lower loft, the ball will fly lower than usual.

In the advanced method, you don't change anything at address. You reduce the effective loft on the club in the swing. What you do is move your weight a little quicker to the left side than usual on the downswing. This puts more weight on your left foot at impact, and your hands will be ahead of the ball, reducing the club's loft. However, with the weight ahead of the ball, you tend to leave the clubface open at impact and push the ball to the right. So, to counteract this tendency, you must roll your right hand over the left a bit as you come through the ball. Then you'll square up the clubface.

43

Into the Wind

Except perhaps for the sand shot, I imagine that hitting into the wind has to be the shot least liked by seniors, indeed, by most amateurs I play with. Most of the time, the wind either makes the ball rise too high in the air and fall far short of where you intended, or it grabs and tosses the ball well to the left or right of target. However, once you understand the reasons for these difficulties, and the correct technique, a headwind won't be as difficult for you.

In playing a shot into the wind, you must appreciate that it will exaggerate every mistake you make. If you hit the ball too hard, and this is the most common fault, you put too much backspin on it, and when the headwind increases the lift on the ball, it soars far too high in the air. If you fade the ball, the wind will turn that fade into a vicious slice. A draw is turned into a vicious hook.

Off the tee, the best strategy for average seniors is simply to make a good solid hit. Do that, and you'll be surprised how little the wind will affect the ball. Concentrate on the back of the ball, and use a smooth, controlled swing, one that won't produce too much backspin. If you're a low-handicapper, try my method, which is basically to play a low shot as previously described. In the downswing, I just move my weight a little more quickly to my left side so that I hit down on the ball a bit harder. I also close the clubface a little coming through impact to counteract the tendency to push the ball to the right.

Into the green, don't make a long loose swing—it will toss the ball up in the air. Instead, play a punch shot (see illustration). Take an iron two clubs stronger than normal and choke down about two inches. Make a very compact backswing, not shifting much weight to the right foot. Grip

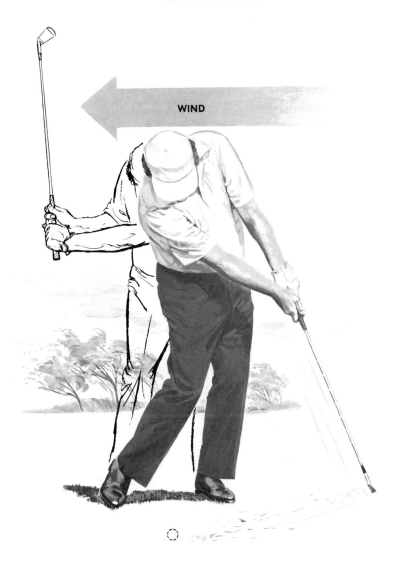

WIND

pressure is key on this shot. Go from a normal grip pressure at address to a very tight grip pressure at impact. This action cuts off the follow-through, keeping the ball low and driving it right through the wind. Because of the headwind, the ball will have enough backspin to stop on the green.

Downwind

Whereas most seniors fear a headwind, hitting a shot downwind, especially a tee shot, is probably among their favorites. Yet, it's surprising how often these shots fail. As with the headwind, you need some understanding in order to be effective.

A following wind has one good effect that is undoubtedly

the reason for its popularity—it straightens out hooks and slices by taking some of the sidespin off the ball. However, it also tends to take backspin off the ball, which therefore won't fly as high as usual, and on iron shots it's more difficult to get enough stop. You can see this effect best in a strong wind, say, over 20 miles an hour, which will actually knock a ball down. Not knowing how to cope with this effect is one reason why you can have problems with downwind shots.

Off the tee, if you merely tee the ball normally and take your usual swing, and assuming a strong wind, the ball will not get up as high as usual, will come to earth sooner, and all other things being equal, you'll lose rather than gain distance. To counteract this, I've found it best to launch the ball at a slightly higher angle. Just tee the ball a little forward in the stance and you'll then catch it a little on the upswing. If you then just swing normally, you'll get your best results. Don't make the mistake of trying to hit much harder than usual in order to take advantage of the wind. Do this, and you'll usually mis-hit the ball, and you'll lose rather than gain distance.

With a strong wind on an approach shot, don't make the mistake of swinging easily, because then you're inviting the "knock down" effect. Remember, you're going to need all the backspin you can get on the shot. If, for example, I had a 150-yard shot, normally a 7-iron for me, I'd take a 9-iron and swing much harder than usual to get the ball well up in the air. You should do the same. If you're in between clubs, you should certainly make a point of picking the weaker club so that you're forced to hit the ball firmly. So take a full swing, a crisp hit, and make a point of finishing very high (see illustration). That will also help you to get the ball up.

47

Try a Long Putter for a Smooth Stroke

Today, many of the Senior Tour players use a long putter, as I do, and a stroke similar to mine. There's even one player on the regular Tour, Mark Lye, who uses a long putter. Although the putter and stroke started out as a method to conquer the "yips," it's now a pretty respectable way to putt. Besides myself, Harold Henning in particular has been very successful with it. If you putt poorly using a conventional stroke, you should think of giving the long putter a try. It's not just for yippers anymore.

Basically, the stroke is like the swing of a pendulum with its center just under the heart. You brace your left hand there against the left side of your chest, holding the end of the putter in a ring formed by your index finger and thumb, as shown. Don't grip too tightly with your left hand—that would restrict the movement. Grip the putter very lightly in your right hand, too. I use what I call a "claw" grip, the grip in between the first two fingers. However, it's not mandatory. I feel the stroke as a swing of the right hand, with the left hand very still. However, in fact, the right arm and shoulder along with the right hand are what swing the club back and through.

This type of stroke helps eliminate the yips for a couple of reasons. With the conventional grip, the hands can fight each other. With the long putter, you stroke with just one hand—the right; the left hand is just a hinge. The yips also are caused by using the smaller muscles of the hands and wrists. Many yippers either use a wristy putting method or else the left wrist breaks down through impact. With the long putter, you don't use the smaller muscles at all. The

stroke is made with the more dependable large muscles, those of the right arm and shoulder. Provided you keep your left hand still, there's nothing in it that can break down. Another advantage of the long putter stroke is that the clubface stays square. In the conventional stroke, you can open and close the blade, and the only way to keep it square is to manipulate the putter with your hands. Finally, you don't have to lean over much. If you're older, or have a bad back, this means you can be comfortable at address and can practice putting without back pain.

BOB ROSBURG

BOB ROSBURG

Born in San Francisco in 1926, Bob Rosburg had an outstanding career in California amateur golf. His most notable victory came in the 1950 Northern California Amateur, when he defeated Ken Venturi. An outstanding infielder in his college days at Stanford, "Rossie" almost chose baseball as a career over golf, but did bring his "baseball" grip to the game at which he was to excel. Turning pro in 1953, he enjoyed success early, winning two events in 1954, and going on to win five more times, his last win coming in 1972 at the age of forty-six. His biggest victory was the 1959 PGA Championship at the Minneapolis Golf Club, St. Louis Park, Minnesota, when he came from nine strokes off the pace after 36 holes to close with brilliant rounds of 68, 66, and win the title by a stroke with a total of 277. He also was a two-time runner-up in the U.S. Open, in 1959 and 1969, and won the Vardon Trophy in 1958 with a stroke average of 70.11. He played on the winning 1959 Ryder Cup team. Rosburg has served as on-course golf analyst for ABC-TV since 1975, and was one of the original seven players involved in the birth of the Senior Tour in 1980. He won the 1981 Legends of Golf with Gene Littler. Despite his commitment to broadcasting, he still finds time to play some ten Senior Tour events a year. Rosburg was always a fader of the ball, with a less than elegant (although highly effective) swing, and his greatest strength is his putting.

Time to Change Your Grip?

When you get to senior status, it's a good idea to review the type of grip you're using. Most golfers use the overlapping grip, also called the Vardon grip, after the old-time great Harry Vardon, and there's no doubt that it is the most popular grip in use today. However, maybe because I've always played with the ten-finger grip, I've realized that the overlap is not necessarily the best grip for all golfers, nor even the best grip for golfers at all stages in their lives.

Everyone today recognizes Jack Nicklaus as the greatest golfer of this era, possibly of all time. Yet the fact that he uses an interlocking grip tends to be overlooked. Tom Kite, one of today's most consistent golfers, also uses this grip. If your fingers are short in relation to the size of your hand, interlocking can be particularly useful, giving you a more flexible and freer wrist cock, and thus more power. I suspect that many of you who fall in this category are struggling along with the overlapping grip, quite unaware that the interlocking grip would suit you much better.

If it's too painful for you to position your left thumb in the conventional position either because of injury or, say, arthritis, then a variation of the standard interlocking grip is a good remedy. Instead of placing the left thumb down the right side of the shaft, take the pressure off the thumb by wrapping it around the grip. This grip was used by Gene Sarazen.

My grip, the ten-finger, tends to be ignored today, because conventional wisdom says that the stronger right

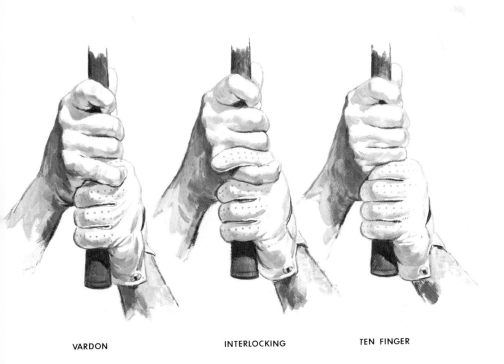

VARDON   INTERLOCKING   TEN FINGER

hand will overpower the left. However, for seniors especially, this argument doesn't cut much ice with me. As you
get older, you tend to lose some hand action and as a result
leave the clubface open through impact, leading to a fade
or slice. The ten-finger grip will encourage stronger hand
action through the ball, and this will square up the
clubface, giving you a straight ball or even a slight draw.
You can gain up to 20 yards off the tee in this way, and
that will help you keep up with the youngsters.

Watch Your Back!

Many young players—both men and women—can finish in what is called the "Reverse C" position. On the downswing, they can drive with the lower body to the left while keeping the head and upper body back behind the ball until well after impact, and finish with the body in a big curve like a backward capital C. They can do this because they're flexible, particularly in the waist area. But what's okay when you're in your twenties or even early thirties can be death to your back when you're a senior.

What often happens is that seniors look at photos or slow-motion videos of these young players, the ones who are presently winning the big tournaments, and think that they should emulate those "Reverse C" finishes. That's wrong. When you try to keep your head and upper body behind the ball into the follow-through, the lack of flexibility in the waist area prevents your lower body from going forward. As a result, you never get your weight through the ball to the left side, and lose power. Worse, you can hurt your lower back with this action, and that is why so many seniors complain of pain in that area.

If you've lost some flexibility through the midsection, forget about the "Reverse C." You must let your whole body—both upper and lower—flow through the ball more on the downswing. You'll be able to keep your chin back of the ball until impact, but after impact, you must let your back release so that you finish with your body erect, and with all your weight on your left foot. If you watch the players of the Senior Tour, either in person or on television, you won't see one that finishes in the "Reverse C."

Rather than falling away from the hole, I'd rather see you falling forward toward the hole, as Gary Player often does because of his extra-strong weight shift. At least your weight will be traveling in the right direction!

"REVERSE C" FINISH   SENIOR FINISH

Vary Your Address

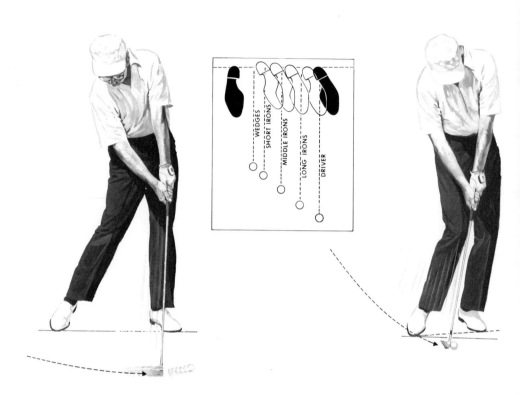

A common problem for many seniors, it seems, is never getting it all together. I'm always hearing something like, "Rossie, I can hit my woods great, but I can't buy a short iron" or just the opposite complaint. If you're having these problems, probably your address is right for the long game, but not for the short, or vice versa. Here's why.

On the woods and longer clubs, you want to drive the ball forward toward the target for distance. Therefore, you need a sweeping, more horizontal hit. At the other end of the set, on the wedges, you want height and plenty of backspin, so the hit should be a steeply descending one, taking a divot after the ball. To accomplish these objectives, you must vary your stance width and ball position.

To set up a sweeping hit on the longer clubs, position your head and body behind the ball, using a wide stance, the insides of your heels about shoulder width apart. The ball position should be forward, up off the left heel, or even the instep, for the driver. On the wedges, take a narrow stance, placing your head and body more over the ball, helping you make a descending blow. Play the ball farther back in the stance, about in the middle. As you move from the driver down to the wedges, gradually narrow your stance by bringing the right foot closer to the left, and gradually notch the ball back from the driver position to the wedge position. Playing the ball back in the stance allows you to catch it earlier in the downswing, which also aids a steeper hit. It's worth adding that, for most golfers, a square stance is best for all clubs except for the short irons, on which you should take an open stance.

When the Ball Is Below

When the ball is below your feet, the first thing to realize is that the general tendency is to fall down the slope, i.e., forward. This means that you never want your weight on your toes; you'll just lose your balance and come across the ball. What you should do is flex your knees at address a little more than usual. In this way, you can have your weight, if anything, favor the heels for maximum stability.

Another problem with this kind of lie is that you're forced to lean over the ball more than usual. One helpful suggestion is to hold the club as close as possible to the end of the grip—without, of course, letting the butt of the left hand be off the club, which would make you lose control. Another is to adjust to the lie as much as possible by flexing the knees rather than leaning over more.

Despite such efforts, you will be leaning over the ball more than usual. This in turn makes you swing on a more upright plane and come through the ball from outside in. As a result, you'll usually fade the ball. Another reason why you'll fade the ball is that, with the ball below your feet, the loft of the club is directed to the right of target. Allow for the fade by aiming left of target; the more severe the lie, the more you should aim to the left.

Always take plenty of club from this type of lie. Then you can swing easily, knowing that you'll reach your target comfortably despite the fade, which doesn't travel as far as a straight shot. If you take too weak a club, you force yourself to swing too hard, and, despite the suggested adjustments, you'll lose your balance. This advice is particularly important on a severe lie. With the ball well below your feet, you must restrict your turn and weight shift in order to retain your balance, and play the shot more with your hands and arms. You won't be able to do that unless you know you have a strong enough club in your hands.

When the Ball Is Above

With the ball above your feet, again gravity will tend to make you lose your balance down the hill—this time, behind you. As a result, almost everything is reversed from the lie below your feet. You have to *avoid* putting too much weight on the heels of the feet, *rather* flexing your knees a little *less* than usual and having your weight favor the *balls* of the feet.

A ball above feet lie will also make you tend to stand more erect than usual. To help you take a more normal address and swing, choke down on the club, the amount depending on the severity of the lie. On a moderate lie, choke down an inch; on a severe lie, as much as three inches.

However, despite these adjustments you'll undoubtedly be standing more erect than usual, which will cause you to swing on a flatter plane. With a flat swing, the tendency is for the clubface to open more rapidly on the backswing and close more quickly through impact, causing you to hook the ball. Again reversing the previous shot, this time at address the loft on the club is directed to the *left* of target; this is another factor that will induce a hook. To allow for the hook, you must aim to the right of target; the more severe the lie, the more you should aim to the right.

One thing that stays the same, however, is that in selecting a club, you should still err on the side of a stronger club. If you take too weak a club, you'll have to swing too hard, and this can make you lose your balance or at best increase the severity of the hook. However, if you know you can easily reach your objective, you can swing more easily and strike the ball more solidly. On very severe lies, you can't make as much turn or shift as much weight back and through as you normally would for fear of losing your balance and missing the ball. So take a much stronger club than usual, and emphasize an easy swing, mostly with your hands and arms.

Play It Smart from Rough

When playing an approach from the rough, you must use your head as well as your best swing. Of course, if you have a perfect lie in the rough so that you can contact the ball cleanly, play the shot normally. However, most of the time it will be impossible to contact the ball cleanly. Some grass will get between the clubhead and the ball at impact,

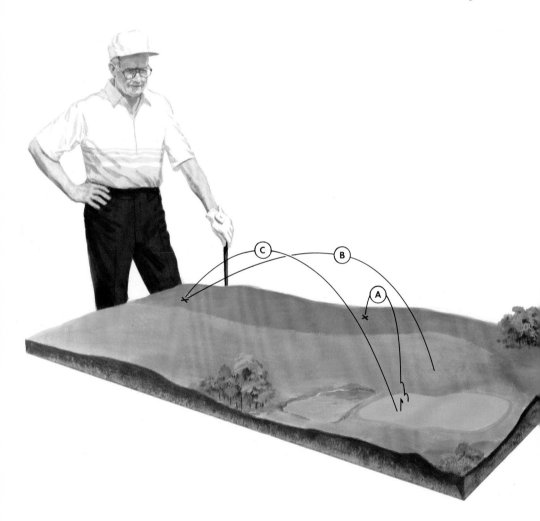

and you won't get the backspin you normally would. As a general rule, you then should allow the ball to land short of the green and roll up to the flag (A).

If you have an obstacle of some sort between your ball and the green, such as a bunker or a pond, as shown here, then going for the green usually will be foolhardy; the ball will probably take one big bounce and go right over the green. In such circumstances, you can save many strokes by laying up to a safe position to one side of the green. Study the terrain carefully, and try to hit to the spot that will leave you the easiest pitch or chip into the green (B).

Sometimes, of course, you can get lucky. If the green is soft (C), or if the green slopes in your favor, then it will hold a shot, even from the rough. Then, by all means fire for the flag.

Downhill at the Back

This is one of the most difficult shots in golf, because you're hitting from what is often a very steep downhill lie, yet you have to get the ball up high enough to clear the lip of the trap.

Before you even attempt the shot, carefully study the height of the lip. If the lip is very high, it may be impossible to get the ball up fast enough to clear the lip. Sometimes, you may be forced to play to one side or other of the direct line to the hole, where the lip is lower. In extreme cases, it pays to play out backward. I remember having to do that several times in my career, especially in Britain, where many of the bunkers are very deep with extremely high lips.

The first adjustment you must make is to set up in such a way that you can swing down parallel to the slope. You want to ensure that your sand wedge will hit down into the sand, not bounce off it into the ball. What you should do is drop your left shoulder so as to square the shoulders to the slope. You'll find that this puts almost all of your weight on your left foot.

At address, open the blade enough to give your shot the height you need, and position your hands ahead of the ball. Open your stance and shoulder alignment so that, on your backswing, you take the club back outside the line and up. There's very little if any turn of the body or weight shift on this shot. You swing the club up almost entirely with your hands, wrists, and arms. On the forward swing, slide your legs through the ball, pulling the club down and through with your left hand so as to keep the clubface open.

Some recommend trying to enter the sand farther behind the ball to allow for the downhill lie. I don't believe in that,

because with extra resistance from the sand, there's more chance of the club opening or closing. Instead, just hit down a normal distance behind the ball; around one and a half inches behind is about the right amount.

Make Your Pitches Count

One of the areas where a senior golfer must shine is in pitching the ball. As one of the older Scottish pros once said to me, "Never forget, laddie, that one of these and one of those counts the same as two of those." In other words, if you can consistently get the ball up and down from within 100 yards of the green, you'll be a match for anyone.

On a normal pitch, you want to strike the ball with a crisp, accelerating, downward hit. To do so, set up with a narrow, open stance and open clubface. Position your hands a little ahead of the ball, with about 65 percent of your weight on your left foot. You should brace your right knee inward and keep it there during the backswing. This keeps the swing compact and helps you start the downswing with your lower body, kicking your right knee through the ball. The narrow stance encourages you to make the swing mostly with your hands and arms; this is correct.

I never try to force a pitch shot, and neither should you. The longest backswing you should take is about three-quarter length, where the hands swing back to shoulder height and through to shoulder height. When you need more swing than that, go to a stronger club. For example, if I had a pitch of one hundred yards, I would never try to hit a sand wedge really hard. Rather, I would take a pitching wedge and make a more controlled swing. Apply the same principle to your pitching game.

In particular, don't make the common mistake of setting up with too wide a stance. Then, you tend to put too much weight on your right foot. This is bad for two reasons. First, your hands are then probably positioned even with the ball or behind it, setting you up for an incorrect, "scooping" action of your right hand through impact.

"Scooping" leads to hitting the ground behind the ball, or hitting up on the ball so that you catch it thin or even top it. Second, too wide a stance encourages too much weight shift and body turn, leading to too long a backswing. You're then forced to decelerate through the ball, and not only won't you hit the ball solidly, you won't get the back-spin you want.

Give My Putting Style a Try

Today, just about the only putting style you see on Tour is the wristless arm-and-shoulder method. This type of stroke is well suited to the beautifully manicured greens the guys and gals presently play. However, not every golfer gets to putt on such greens. For example, if you play on Bermuda greens, which often are very grainy, or if the grass is not cut low, then my putting style, which involves a wristy, "rapping" type of hit, will serve you better.

This style has other advantages. I tried the arm-and-shoulder method at one time, and found that I tended to take too long a backswing and then decelerated through the ball. It was as though I had no "hit" when I got back to the ball, and my putting suffered. From what I see, this happens to many amateurs, too. In contrast, I could always hit the ball crisply with the "rapping" style, and make a good, accelerating stroke. I think you will, too.

If you want to try my style, get a putter with a little loft. You're going to hit down on the ball with the hands slightly ahead. So you need a putter with about three or four degrees of loft to get the ball up and rolling on top of the grass. I personally use a slightly open stance, but it's not essential; use a square stance if you prefer it. I do recommend setting slightly more weight on the left foot. This helps you hit down, and having the weight more on one foot tends to prevent a sway. To encourage a wristy stroke, I carry my hands low, and while I still use a ten-finger grip, I turn both hands slightly outward from the normal grip so that the back of the left hand and palm of the right are square to the intended line to the hole. At address, both arms touch my body, my left hand barely touching my left leg. On a short- or medium-length putt, the arms don't move much, and the hands don't move sideways to the right or left. I just hinge my wrists, which technically shuts the blade. I work the blade from shut going back to open in the follow-through, but actually this keeps it square to the target line throughout the stroke. I then hit down on the ball, giving a smart "rap," with little or no follow-through. Only if I have a long putt do I use my arms to give me the necessary distance.

The way I putt the ball is similar to hitting a nail with a hammer. You don't take a hammer all the way back and ease into the hit. You take it back with the wrists, then give the nail a crack. It is, I feel, a very natural way to putt. By the way, I use the same method in chipping except that I play the ball back a little more in the stance. So, if you like my putting style, by all means try it in chipping, too.

DAVE MARR

DAVE MARR

Born in Houston, Texas, in 1933, Dave Marr was exposed to the game by his father, Dave Marr, Sr., a Houston golf professional. In the 1950s, Marr had the good fortune to work for Claude Harmon at Winged Foot. At the time, a job with Harmon was like attending a finishing school for the Tour, and in 1960, Marr "graduated" and started on a successful playing career. Sam Snead once said that Marr made the most of what he had. He certainly did. He was —and is—a model swinger of the club, and in particular a marvelous wood player, a fine bunker player, and an excellent putter. Marr's greatest moment came in 1965 when he won the PGA Championship at the tough Laurel Valley Golf Club, Ligonier, Pennsylvania, with a four-under-par 280. He played on that year's Ryder Cup team and was PGA Player of the Year. He also won three other Tour events. Television came into Marr's life when, as the PGA Tournament Committee Chairman in the mid-1960s, he was instrumental in developing the television network arrangements that gave tournament golf its initial exposure. In 1973, Marr was invited to join ABC as a golf announcer. His perceptive and witty commentary have been part of the golf scene ever since.

Everyman's Warmup

I'm not going to spend much time impressing on you the importance of a warmup before playing golf. You know it as well as I do: In every sport, from tennis to Ping-Pong, you'd warm up before a match, but somehow in golf, many seniors just walk to the first tee and take a big rip at the ball —and hurt themselves! What I am going to suggest could be called the lazy man's warmup or, come to think of it, Everyman's warmup.

Step One: To get your golf muscles moving, put a club behind your back, as shown, and start turning very gently to the right and left. Don't force the big turn right away! Start with quarter-turns, and work up to full turns.

Step Two: Put a doughnut-type weight on your driver and take some easy swings. Swing back and forth continuously until your golf muscles are as limber as possible. Warning: Never swing at full speed with the weight on the club—you want to warm up your muscles, not tear them! By the way, I don't advocate swinging two or three clubs at a time, as is often suggested, because you're not using your regular grip.

Step Three: Take a few full swings with the club you're going to use from the first tee, usually the driver. Make these practice swings as realistic as possible. Aim at a target in the distance as you would on a real shot. Also, use a substitute for the ball—a flower or a tee stuck in the ground.

If you have a little additional time, take a wedge and chip some balls, again to a "target" patch of grass, in the area around the tee. Also, putt a few balls to a tee.

Lastly, to go along with the lazy man's warmup, I'm going to sneak in just one lazy man's exercise. In golf, as in

every sport, the legs are the first to go. That's why so many seniors don't putt and chip as well as they once did—the legs, which are their foundation, are not as steady as they once were. With golf cars the rule at so many courses these days, you must do something for your legs. I do toe raises in the shower—they're terrific. Stand with your feet together and rise onto your toes and down again twenty times, holding the last rise for, say, ten seconds. I guarantee you'll feel some heat there in the calves, thighs, fanny, and stomach!

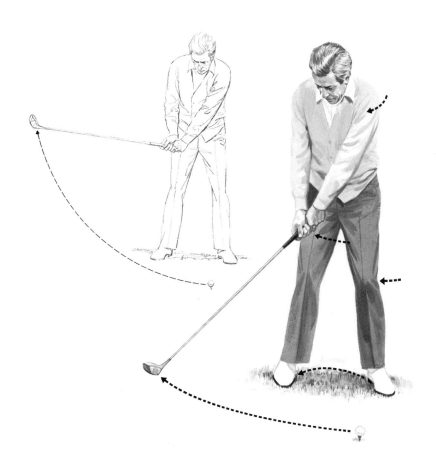

Cure for a Fast Backswing

You've heard this one before, I'm sure! You're having a particularly bad day, and one of your friends, taking pity on you, volunteers what seems like useful information: "You're swinging too fast today." So you try to swing slower, but your drives still head for the boondocks and he still says you're swinging too fast! Frustrating, right? Now, your friend is correct in a way—it does look like you're swinging too fast. However, the fast swing is just the result. The cause is overactive hands in the takeaway.

What is happening is that, as you swing back, you break the wrists right off the ball, straight up (small illustration). When you do that, you can't make a full turn of your shoulders, you don't use your legs, and you never shift your weight to your right foot. In short, you never get a full windup. This "pickup action," as it's often called, looks fast because it's so abbreviated. Now, I'm not a kinesiologist, but I know for a fact that you can't move the big muscles of the body as fast as you can the hands and wrists. So, to slow down the swing, you've got to involve your body right at the start.

The cure for your problem is what is often called the one-piece takeaway. However, seniors especially must use the right type of one-piece takeaway. Many of you think that if you swing the arms and club, along with turning your shoulders, it will do the trick. When you were younger, this probably was enough to set the lower body in motion. However, as you get older, your legs often don't work as well as they once did. So, as a senior, you've got to get them into motion at the same time as the body. Okay?

The right sort of takeaway for a senior feels as though you're taking everything back together. Your one-piece takeaway blends the breaking of the wrists, swinging the arms and club away, turning the shoulders, and starting the hip turn and the weight shift to the inside of the right foot. The large illustration shows exactly what I mean.

To correct the quick pickup, get in front of a full-length mirror and imitate my action. Go from address to the correct takeaway position, say, a dozen times a day. You'll soon make the one-piece takeaway a habit.

79

The Feet-Together Drill

The most valuable, versatile swing drill I know of is to practice with the feet together. It teaches you a pure swinging action with good balance and rhythm, the fullest use of the body, and the strong release that is the hallmark of a good player. It also helps you cure many of the swing faults that seniors suffer from. I first learned the drill from George Fazio thirty-five years ago, and ever since I've made a point of including it in every practice session when I want to work on my swing. You should, too.

Use a short iron such as a 7-iron, stand with your feet just a few inches apart, and warm up. Start with little quarter-swings, and gradually work up to half-, three-quarter, and full swings. The unusual stance will feel awkward at first, so you should put the ball on a low tee initially until you're confident you can meet it solidly. Once you're comfortable with the drill, graduate to the 5-iron, a great all-around club with which to practice the swing.

One of the most important lessons the feet-together drill will teach you is the sensation of using your whole body. The narrower your stance, the more you can turn the body, and this drill provides the ultimate narrow stance. It also aids your footwork, especially if you practice it occasionally in street shoes. Many seniors, I notice, take a stance, dig in with their spikes, then lock the lower body and never use it in the swing. The drill makes good use of the legs and feet a habit. Another important feature is that the narrow stance prevents you from making any jerky

moves, hitting too hard, or muscling the ball from the
upper arms or shoulders. If you do, you'll literally fall over.
To keep your balance, you have to truly *swing* the club
back and through. You'll also discover out how hard you
can swing without forcing, and thus losing the swing—a
valuable lesson.

Stopping the Sway

A very common fault among seniors is swaying. At the top of the swing, your weight has moved to the *outside* of the right foot, and often your right knee collapses and is outside your right foot (small illustration). With your weight so far to the right, your weight shift back to the left foot is delayed. In the meantime, you either hit from the top with your hands or you come over the ball with your right shoulder and swing through the ball from out to in. When you sway, you invite a lot of "strangers" into your swing—you can slice, hit the ball fat, or even duck-hook it. Here's the cure.

The first thing to do is look at your feet. The prime cause of a sway is setting your right foot in a position where it's splayed out to the right. This encourages too much of a weight shift, and you sway. Most of the seniors who have this fault walk with their feet naturally turned out. So, if this is your natural tendency, be aware of it and at address take care to set your right foot square to your target line (large illustration). This correction by itself will often cure the sway, as it tends to brace the right leg inward at address, keeping the right leg firm in the backswing.

Unfortunately, squaring your right foot is not an infallible cure, because you could still address the ball with what might be termed "slack" legs. In other words, both legs, instead of being set in the correct knock-kneed position, would appear almost straight in a mirror in front of you. In this position, your leg muscles are not activated and the right knee can still wind up outside the right foot at the top. What you must do is set both knees slightly inward—a good model in this respect is the slightly knock-kneed stance of Gary Player. Setting the right knee inward braces the leg so that, when you shift the weight to the right foot

on the backswing, it resists sideways movement. At the top of the swing, the weight is then on the *inside* of the right foot, as it should be. Setting the left knee inward makes it break toward the ball and to the right. This is correct.

It's worth adding that, if you shift into a braced right leg, the leg unwinds first in the downswing so that you get the correct lower-body lead and a delayed, powerful hit.

The Long Explosion Shot

I see a lot of seniors go into a bunker to play a long explosion shot, bury their feet in the sand over their shoe tops, and take a jerky, heaving swing, apparently trying to remove all the sand from the bunker! You displace a lot of sand that way, but only move it and the ball a short distance. Usually, the ball never gets out of the bunker. In contrast, if you watch good bunker players like Sam Snead or Ben Crenshaw play the shot, they almost tiptoe in and swing as though in their sleep. They use finesse, not force, to get the necessary distance, and so should you.

If you use a very open stance and blade on short sand shots and put your weight left, as is often advocated, it makes for an abrupt up-and-down V-shaped swing. On the long explosion shot, you must adjust the swing to one much nearer a normal wedge shot from the fairway. In other words, you'd only open the blade a trifle, take only a very slightly open stance, and play the ball back farther, between the middle of the stance and the left heel (large illustration). Since the blade is less open, you'll hit the ball lower and longer, and because the ball position, stance, and weight distribution are near normal, you'll make a wider, more U-shaped swing (small illustration); this also will drive the ball forward more than the V-shaped swing.

Personally, I never was one for opening the face of a sand wedge on short sand shots, preferring to keep the clubface squarely at the target, and relying on a sand wedge with plenty of bounce to give me the needed "skidding" action. (Bounce is the amount that the sole of the sand wedge angles down from the leading edge to the back.) I found this a lot easier than using a very open blade, and, if you do too, then you don't have to adjust the blade on longer shots. All you have to do is square up your stance until it is slightly open as described above.

As a rule, it's best to enter the sand your normal distance behind the ball, about two inches or so. However, there's a limit to the distance you can hit a ball taking this much sand. When you reach that limit, enter the sand closer to the ball, but be careful to guard against catching the ball clean by keeping your eyes on the entry point until well past impact.

Uphill in the Front

If you catch an uphill lie in a greenside bunker, the most important point is to set your shoulders on the same plane as the slope (small illustration). This allows you to swing through the ball parallel to the slope, hitting the divot of sand—and the ball—out of the bunker. Don't take your normal stance. If you set up with the body vertical, you'll just stick your club in the bank of sand. You'll only move the sand a couple of feet, and that's how far you'll move the ball, too!

The good news on the uphill sand shot is that if you're close to the pin the ball will come out high and land softly. The bad news is that, if you're a long way from the pin, it's difficult to judge the distance. The harder you hit the ball, it seems, the higher it goes, but it doesn't go much farther, because, with your shoulders on the same plane as the slope, you've increased the effective loft on the sand wedge. On longer shots, you really have to hit much harder than usual. However, always plan to enter the sand your normal distance behind the ball—you'll be more consistent this way.

When you need more distance from an uphill lie in grass, going to a less lofted club such as a pitching wedge or a 9-iron can be a good idea. But I wouldn't recommend selecting these clubs from a bunker, since they usually don't have any bounce and could stick in the sand. You need the bounce on the sand wedge so that it skids through the sand and takes a shallow cut. If you normally open the sand wedge on short shots and use a wedge with little bounce, use a squarer face if you need more distance, but leave it a trifle open so you still have enough bounce. If your wedge has plenty of bounce, as mine does, square it right at the hole.

86

If you're on a very steep uphill lie, you won't be able to set your shoulders exactly on plane to the slope, because this would put too much weight on your right foot, and you'd lose your balance. Then, you must bend your left knee a little more than usual for good balance (large illustration).

If you have a particularly good lie, the lip is low, but the pin is back, chipping the ball can give you the needed distance. Take a sand wedge or pitching wedge and adjust to the slope as described above. But, play the ball back in the stance this time so that you catch the ball first.

Blocked Backswing

Every once in a while, you're going to have a problem such as the one depicted here (large illustration). A bush or other obstacle in the rough blocks your backswing. If you really have no backswing at all in the direction you want to go, then you must take your licking, and simply chip the ball out sideways and back into play. Your first priority must be to get out of trouble, and place the ball so as to set up your next shot. Like a player in chess or checkers, always think one shot ahead.

Often you can contrive some sort of backswing if you narrow the arc of the swing. The first adjustment is to take a short, well-lofted club like an 8-iron. I see too many seniors in such circumstances taking too long a club with too little loft. This is wrong not only because the long club will hit the bush. The small amount of loft prevents you from making the second adjustment, which is to play the ball back in your stance, but leaving the hands ahead (illustration below). This makes the swing narrower, since the club will swing up more abruptly. However, playing the ball back also reduces the effective loft on the club to that of, say, a 4-iron. So, if you take a 4-iron and then play it back, you'll have no loft at all to get the ball up and out of the rough! As my British colleagues would say, I'll draw a merciful veil over the results of that endeavor!

You'll probably need to make two further adjustments. One is to place more weight on the left foot. Like playing the ball back, this will narrow the swing by taking the club back more steeply. The other is to choke down on the club (upper illustration), which simply reduces the width of the arc.

When you have a lie like this, be prepared to take your time setting up. You're going to have to experiment a little, as I'm doing in the largest illustration, to tailor the adjustments to the particular lie. Try some practice backswings. You may find, for example, that you want to choke down more or less, or play the ball back farther or less far than you first planned.

Then go ahead and swing. You may not be able to reach the green, but hopefully you'll advance your ball to where your next shot will be an easy one.

Accelerate Through on the Green, Too

From what I've seen, seniors miss more putts because of timidity than for any other reason. As you come into impact, you get "careful," and the result is a lack of "hit" in the stroke, a lack of acceleration, and you leave the ball short of the hole. Another fault that gives you a similar result is taking too long a backswing. Then you subconsciously realize that if you make a good accelerating stroke through, you'll go too far past the hole. So you decelerate instead. Usually you overcompensate, slow down too much, and again leave the ball short. If these are your problems, here's the solution.

For most golfers, the right hand supplies the power in the stroke. To overcome a weak hit, therefore, you need to work on your right hand. The best way to do this is to practice stroking some putts with only your right hand on the club (larger illustration). With this method, you'll quickly detect timid hits or too long a backswing, and soon you'll be taking the correct, usually shorter, length of backswing and accelerating through. When you're again hitting the ball solidly, you'll hear a crisper sound at impact. That's good. Tuck it away in your memory for future reference.

If you need a little more help, then look at the smaller illustration. To accelerate through the ball, it helps to imagine a tack in the back of the ball, and that you're going to drive the tack into the ball at impact with your right hand. Jack Burke told me that, and he was a great putter.

You'll notice I'm practicing short putts. This is very important. Too many seniors practice fifty-foot putts. How

many of those are you going to hole? If you can stop the ball within three feet of the cup, that's great! It's okay to hit a few of these for feel, but devote most of your practice putting time to short putts, the ones you have a chance to make. All the great players I've seen were experts in cleaning up the "trash"—the putts from six feet in. Those are the ones to practice. Start at three feet from the hole and work out to six feet. You'll hole a lot of putts, build up your stroke, and really boost your confidence.

Spot Your Putts

A very common putting problem, especially among seniors, is misaiming the putt. In other words, you never get the blade of the putter squarely aligned to your intended line. Most people tend to aim well to the right of the line. As a result, they have to loop the putter back "over the top," so to speak, and pull it back into the hole. But I've also seen a few who aim left of the hole! A kindred problem, particularly if you have lost a little sharpness of eye, is "losing" your line. What I mean by that is that you get down behind the ball to read the break, you see the line, but by the time you've come into the ball from the side and taken your stance, the line is unclear to you. To cure both problems, I suggest you "spot" your putts.

The first spot you need—the aiming spot (see illustration)—is one just in front of the ball. When you're reading the break from behind the ball, pick out a spot about a foot in front of the ball. This could be a piece of dead grass or other discolored piece of grass. Keep your eyes on this spot as you walk to the side and step into the ball. Set the putter face squarely at the spot, which you know is on the line, then take your stance. When you make your stroke, make a point of swinging the putter through toward the spot.

A second spot is necessary only if there's a break on the putt. If you read the putt as, say, a three-foot break to the right, also pick out a "target" spot—again this could be a piece of dead or discolored grass—three feet to the left of the hole. Now, when you stroke the putt, you follow through to the aiming spot with the thought of leaving the ball at your target spot. If your calculations and strength are right, the ball will take the break and feed right into the hole.

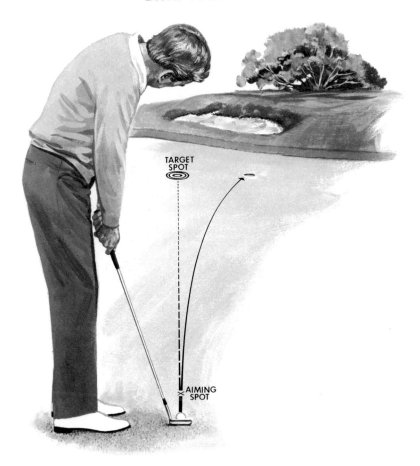

With this method, every putt is visualized and stroked as though it were a *straight* putt, which I think you'll find a lot easier than trying to visualize the curving path of a breaking putt. You have to find your own way, of course. However, I think a lot of putts are missed at the moment of truth—impact—because you push the ball to make certain it breaks to the right or pull it to make certain it breaks to the left!

Try the "two spot" system. Once you get used to it, you'll like it a lot.

DOUG SANDERS

DOUG SANDERS

Born in Cedartown, Georgia, in 1933, Doug Sanders developed his unique style—an extra-wide stance, and a very short swing—out of necessity. As a caddie at the Cherokee G & C C in Cedartown, he wasn't allowed to play and had to sneak out on the course. The hole the caddies played, he says, was so narrow, "I developed a short swing so as not to lose any golf balls." It certainly has served him well, and he developed into a gifted shotmaker, especially known for his low wind-cheaters. He was—and still is—famed for his colorful outfits. As an amateur, Sanders won the 1951 Jaycee Junior, the 1953 Southeastern Amateur, and the 1955 Mexican "World" and All-American Championships. He also won the 1956 Canadian Open, the first amateur to do so. As a pro, Sanders won twenty Tour events through 1972, and was a Ryder Cup team member in 1967. His best year was 1961, when he won five tournaments. In the majors, Sanders finished second in the 1959 PGA, the 1961 U.S. Open, and the 1966 and 1970 British Opens. As a senior, Sanders won the 1983 World Seniors, and is host at the Senior Tour's Doug Sanders Kingwood Celebrity Classic near Houston, Texas.

97

Beat the "Freezes"

A good golf swing is a thing of beauty—graceful, powerful, fluid. It can't be a herky-jerky, stop-and-start motion. I see a lot of seniors coming to a dead stop before starting to swing; the result is that their muscles tighten, and it's almost impossible to make a good pass at the ball.

You freeze because you don't have what pros call a good pre-swing routine, an unvarying step-by-step method of taking address. In fact, many of you seldom set up the same way twice. Consequently, you're never certain that your aim is correct, your alignment is correct, or that you're even the right distance away from the ball.

Although better golfers' routines differ slightly, here are the things that practically all of them do. Step One is to take your grip, starting from behind the ball. This viewpoint allows you to identify your target line and visualize the type of shot you want. Then select a spot on the target line about two feet in front of the ball—a piece of discolored grass, something that stands out. If you keep your eyes on this spot as you move to the side of the ball, you'll find it easy to square the clubface to the "short line" from ball to spot. Best of all, you'll know it's square. Step Two is to step into the ball and measure to it, your right foot leading. Then put your feet together so that a line across your toes is parallel to your "short line." From this position, you'll find it easy to spread your feet (Step Three), first the left, positioning the ball correctly in relation to the foot, and then the right, checking that a line across your toes also is parallel to your "short line."

Having taken your address (Step Four), waggle the club to break up tension and keep in motion. Take one or two waggles—the number is your choice—but always take the same number of waggles. Then, use a "trigger" to smoothly set your swing in motion. Basically, this is a little shift of weight to the left foot and back to the right as you start the swing. You can do this in many ways—with your hands, your right knee, or with a twist of the hips, for example. Find your best "trigger," then stick to it.

Once you've developed your routine, never vary it. You won't freeze again, and you'll give yourself the best chance of making a good, fluid swing.

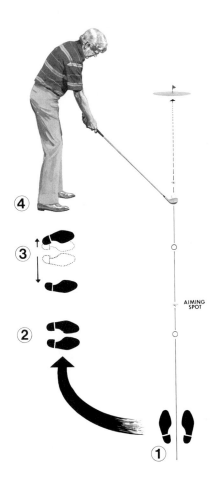

Tuck the Right Arm In

In golf, the apparent cause of a problem is often only a symptom. To find the true cause, you really have to dig for it. A short time ago, I was playing in a pro-am and one of my partners, a high-handicapper, was pull/slicing every shot. He needed help, obviously, but he'd tried most of the obvious things, such as checking his clubface aim, his ball position, and whether his feet were square to the target line (small illustration).

The low-handicapper in the group pointed out that the high-handicapper was swinging back outside the target line, and then coming over the top from out to in. He added that, although his feet were square to the line at address, his shoulders were very open, pointing to the left of parallel to the target line. "Open shoulders," he said, "lead to an out-to-in swing."

That was very true, I thought, as far as it went. But another look at the high-handicapper made it clear to me that we needed to go deeper than that. I noticed that at address, his right arm was almost straight, and this was forcing the right shoulder forward, in turn twisting the shoulders into an open position. I also saw the root cause of his trouble—his weak grip, the hands turned very much to the left, the V's pointing up at his left cheek.

The position of your arms is largely decided by the type of grip you take. If you take a very weak grip, you're almost forced into an address such as the high-handicapper took—right arm straight and out from the body, left arm forced in and shoulders open. The opposite is true with a very strong grip, the hands turned very much to the right, and the V's pointing up outside the right shoulder; the left arm moves away from the body, and the right arm tucks into the body. The correction actually started with a stronger grip. Then it was easy for him to position the arms correctly and square up the shoulders (large illustration).

There are two morals to this story: (1) Very often, our "swing faults" are in reality address faults. (2) If you can't identify your problem quickly, run, don't walk, to your friendly PGA pro. The fault may be more deep-seated than any of your friends—even a low-handicapper—could realize.

Swing a Heavy Club

A lot of seniors ask me what exercises I recommend. I think they expect me to list a series of exercises, and seem surprised when I just tell them to go out and buy a heavy driver—such clubs are available through your golf professional's shop—and use it. (A good alternative is to get a doughnut-shaped weight and put it on an old driver, and

swing that.) Yet this one exercise is all you need.

Swing a heavy club back and through a few times, and its first benefit is immediately apparent—it slows down your swing. One of the most common faults among seniors is swinging back too fast. Very often, this is caused by the hands and wrists dominating the action in the takeaway— the wrists take the club up steeply and you usually don't make a full body turn. With the heavy club, you can't swing back too fast. This is because its weight forces you to take the club back using your arms and turning your shoulders and hips. In short, you're forced to make a correct "one piece" takeaway, sweeping the club away from the ball, and make a solid turn and full windup for maximum power.

The second benefit of swinging the heavy club follows hard on the heels of the first—its weight forces you to swing the whole club through the ball (see illustration) into a full finish. When you start down, its weight forces you to pull it down with the big muscles of the lower body leading, the move that leads to a late, powerful hit. This corrects a common mistake among seniors of "hitting from the top," that is, throwing the clubhead at the ball from the top of the swing. Hitting too early makes the club go outside the line on the way down, causing a slice. Also, with the wrists uncocked well before impact, you lose a lot of power.

But that's not all. Swinging the heavy club keeps your golf muscles strong and limber, and helps you retain or even increase your range of motion, valuable benefits for all seniors. Lastly, unlike conventional exercises, which many golfers soon find boring and abandon, swinging the heavy club is fun. It's not a problem to do it for, say, five minutes each day—all you need.

Make the Wind Your Friend

Many senior amateurs, I notice, are completely thrown by a strong crosswind. You get to swinging too hard and make a lot of mistakes—and high numbers. Instead, make the crosswind your friend; you'll get far better results. Don't try to fight it unless you're a low-handicapper.

Whatever your skill level, the first thing to do is make certain you have enough club in your hand. Swing too hard and you mis-hit the ball because subconsciously, you realize you've taken too little club. If you happen to catch the ball flush, then too hard a swing puts too much backspin on the ball, and it gets up too high.

If you normally hit the ball fairly straight, the easiest way to handle crosswinds is to allow the wind to blow the ball into the target (see illustration). Figure out how much it will blow the ball to the right or left, and hit toward an imaginary target that far to the side of the actual target; nature will do the rest.

However, if your normal ball flight is a slice, then you must realize it will "fight" a right to left wind. The wind will tend to neutralize your slice, and the ball will fly straighter than usual. Depending on the force of the wind and the amount of your normal slice, the ball will slice less or even fly dead straight. So aim less far to the right, or even right at the actual target. Because your ball will "fight" the wind, take a much stronger club than usual. A left to right wind, however, will be working with your slice, and you should aim farther left of target than on a calm day. The same applies to those who hook the ball, but in reverse.

If you have the skill, you may want to fight the wind, especially into the green, because the ball will stop where

it lands. On a left to right wind, aim right at the flag, and let your right hand roll over your left at impact, creating a hook that will hold the ball straight. On a right to left wind, pull across the ball with your left hand, holding the ball straight with a slice.

Ball Above in the Bunker

When your ball lies above your feet in the sand, you must guard against digging into the side of the bunker too deeply, the most common error. It's all too easy for the club to enter the sand too far behind the ball and stick there, not generating enough force to get the ball out.

To ensure that the club doesn't dig too much, make

several adjustments to the technique you'd use for a sand shot from a level lie. First, choke down on the club enough to compensate for the amount the ball lies above the feet. Second, avoid the mistake of digging the feet too much into the sand; that would put your feet even farther below the ball, making the shot even more difficult. Work your feet in just deep enough to get a solid stance. Third, make certain that you open the clubface before taking your grip. With the face open, the flange on the back of the sand wedge will strike the sand before the leading edge, ensuring that the club takes a shallow cut. If the clubface were square, the club would cut down into the sand—the opposite of what you want.

Don't try to reduce the risk of digging by hitting the sand closer to the ball. Because of the slope, the heel of the wedge won't strike the sand first as it would when you open the clubface on a level lie. Only the toe will cut through the sand, and you'll take less sand than usual, often causing you to thin the ball and fly it over the green. Instead, you should aim to enter the sand *farther* behind the ball than usual, say, two inches behind rather than one inch.

Using a sand wedge from this type of lie, you're going to pull the ball rather than hook it as you would with a less lofted club. The more the ball is above your feet, the greater the pull. Aim to the right of the hole to allow for it. Choking down on the club helps, provided that you also stand a little closer to the ball, allowing you to take the club up a trifle more steeply. If you were to stand the same distance from the ball as you would on a level lie, you'd swing on too flat a plane and exaggerate the pull.

The Divot Hole Shot

Fortunately, it doesn't happen very often. You hit a great drive, right down the middle of the fairway, and land up in someone else's divot hole. However, when it does happen to you, you must be prepared mentally as well as physically.

On the mental side, don't give way to anger or start moaning about "bad luck" or the poor condition of the course. Those old Scots who invented the game never intended it to be completely fair. Bad lies are part of golf, and you must accept them. On the physical side, be prepared to play the shot a little differently from usual.

The biggest mistake I see is attempting to hit the shot with a normal swing. You must appreciate that the ball is sitting lower than usual, below the surface of the grass. You must somehow get down to ball level.

If you attempt to swing normally, you'll take the club away low in the takeaway, and when you come through the ball, the angle on which the club will descend won't be steep enough. You'll hit through the ball with more of a sweeping blow and probably you'll hit it thin. You could even catch the back end of the divot hole, ruining the shot.

To hit down steeply, the first adjustment is to play the ball back a couple of inches in the stance. However, keep your hands in their regular position, about opposite the inside of the left thigh. They then will be well ahead of the ball. The result is that you catch the ball while the clubhead is still descending.

Second, you also need a more upright swing. To do that, break the wrists a little faster in the takeaway, taking the club up more steeply. In the downswing, pull down strongly with the left hand into and through the ball.

I can't stress enough that you must be sure you have enough club in your hands to easily make the required distance. You'll need a precise hit to take the ball first and then the dirt. Swing deliberately, well within yourself. You can't do that if you know that the only way you can get the ball to the target with the club you've selected is to hit very hard!

Water? Just Skip It!

Nine times out of ten, if you found your ball in the situation depicted in the illustration, the smart play would be to chip out to the fairway and try to get down in a pitch and a putt. This would certainly be true just about every time in stroke play and most of the time in match play. But, if you're down in a match, and the loss of the hole in question would mean the loss of the match, then hitting the ball low under the tree branches so that it skips across the water like a flat stone can be not only the best shot to play, it may be the only way you can put the ball on the green.

If you've never practiced this shot before, and there are not many people who have, the first step is to use your imagination. Pick out a spot in the water from which the ball will make its first skip, then visualize the next skip, and so on, including the ball's subsequent run up the bank and onto the green.

In selecting a club, you obviously need the trajectory of about a 3-iron to keep the ball low under the tree branches. However, I wouldn't suggest you actually use a long iron here. You want to make quite certain that you catch the ball first, then take a divot. You should play the ball back a couple of inches in the stance from its normal position, leaving the hands ahead of the ball. In this way, you're set up to hit the ball as the clubhead is still descending. With the hands ahead, you hood or deloft the club somewhat. This means that if you took a long iron, you would reduce its effective loft to zero! To allow for delofting, select about a 5-iron.

The type of swing you use also is very important. Don't make a long, wristy swing—it would throw the ball up in the air. Instead, keep the ball low with a short, brisk, punch-type action. Grip the club rather firmly, take a short backswing, then hit down on the ball. Your left hand must lead the clubhead through the ball so that the right hand never rolls over the left. If it did, you'd put hook spin on the ball and it would dive into the water and go right to the bottom. However, if you hit the ball flush and your calculations are correct, it will skip across the water and onto the green. And won't your opponent howl!

The 3-Wood Chip

A tough situation for the average senior is to have the ball roll through a green and into a bad lie in the rough. If you try to chip the ball, you never quite know what will happen when the club hits the high grass. One time the grass could slow the club down, dumping the ball short of the hole. Another time you could hit harder, trying to allow for the resistance of the grass, it wouldn't materialize, and you would send the ball too far. If this shot has proved a problem for you, then try playing it the way I do—with a 3-wood.

The rationale behind using a fairway wood is the same as when hitting a longer shot from the rough. If you try to use a long iron, the hosel of the club can catch in the grass, closing the face and ruining the shot. But you do far better with a fairway wood, because a wood tends to part the grass, gliding through it. The same thing happens on a short shot from rough—the 3-wood glides through, making for a far more certain result.

Choke down on the 3-wood for control, take a narrow stance, and play the ball a little forward of center. In the swing, you never pick the club up. You just sweep it back and through. You'll find that the ball rolls right through the rough and out onto the green. After you've tried the shot a couple of times, you'll appreciate that the best thing about it is its safety. You can even hit the ball a little heavy or fat, and it still rolls through up to the hole.

I use the 3-wood shot mostly when I have to go through up to about three or four feet of rough by the green. If you have more rough than that to traverse, then you'll have to pitch or chip the ball. Another time I like to use my 3-wood is when the ball lies on the fringe, but against the collar of the rough. Many suggest hitting the ball at the equator with the sand wedge in these circumstances, but I get better results with my 3-wood and I think you will, too.

I'll tell you one thing. I'll back myself using my 3-wood on this shot against anyone using any other club. In fact, I've won quite a bit of money that way! Try it. You're going to like it.

The Texas Wedge

At one time, I think it would be fair to say that either amateurs did not use the putter from the fringe, what's called the Texas Wedge shot, or certainly didn't use it enough. They invariably chipped the ball from the fringe, and often when using their putter would have been far safer. However, today I think the boot is on the other foot. From what I see in pro-ams, senior amateurs seem to use their putters from off the green all the time. They've taken Arnold Palmer's sound advice—that your worst putt from the fringe will often be as good as your best chip—too much to heart. In short, they're overusing the shot.

The reason the Texas Wedge can be a marvelous stroke saver is the loft on the putter. Everyone knows that it's easier to hit a chip solidly with a 4-iron than with a sand wedge. So, it follows that it's easier to hit the ball solidly with a putter than even a 4-iron. However, the putter's lack of loft can be a problem in certain situations from the fringe. The trick is to know when your best percentage shot is the Texas Wedge, and when it's safer to chip.

If your ball lies very close to the green, say within two feet or so, if the fringe is clipped very short and is very smooth, then by all means play the Texas Wedge. Use it also if the grass in the fringe is very thin, or from a bare lie, when it is so easy to stub a chip shot. When the grain of the grass is with you, that is, growing in the direction in which you want to send the ball, then again use the Texas Wedge.

However, if the ball is lying farther than two feet away from the green, it's usually safer to chip the ball. Remember: The farther the ball is from the green, the more difficult it becomes to judge how hard you should hit it to roll it through the fringe. Don't use the Texas Wedge if the ball

114

is down in the grass. If you do, the ball will bounce and won't roll the right distance. You also shouldn't use it if the grass is heavy—again the ball will bounce on you, with inconsistent results. Finally, if the grain of the grass is against you, then chip, hitting a little more firmly than usual.

TOMMY AARON

TOMMY AARON

Born in Gainesville, Georgia, in 1937, Tommy Aaron had an outstanding amateur career in the 1950s, winning the Georgia and Southeastern amateurs twice each and the Georgia Open three times. He went to the final of the 1958 U.S. Amateur, losing to Charlie Coe, but won important amateur events such as the 1959 Sunnehanna and 1960 Western Amateurs, and was a member of the winning 1959 Walker Cup team. Joining the PGA Tour in 1961, Aaron soon developed the reputation of being a perennial "bridesmaid," finishing second nine times before breaking through to his first victory, a playoff win over Sam Snead in the 1969 Canadian Open. The high point in his career was his victory in the 1973 Masters, where he left J. C. Snead one stroke behind and Jack Nicklaus two strokes behind. He was the first native Georgian to win. Aaron twice played for the United States in Ryder Cup play, in 1969 and 1973. Aaron joined the Senior Tour in 1987. His highest finish has been a second place with Lou Graham in the 1988 Legends of Golf, when the pair lost in a six-hole playoff to Orville Moody and Bruce Crampton.

The Baseball Drill

If there's one most common fault among seniors I've played with, it's slicing the ball. Slicing is a serious problem for any golfer, but for seniors it's especially damaging, because a slice simply doesn't go as far as a straight ball. In fact, for most seniors, a draw is the best shape of shot, as you'll get more distance with a draw than even a straight shot.

The reason for slicing is very simple—at impact the clubface is open in relation to the swing path through the ball. This can be caused by faults I'll deal with in the next two lessons: too tight a grip, too weak a grip, and incorrect ball position and body alignment. Another very important cause is poor rotation of the hands and arms in the hitting area.

To draw the ball, the hands and arms should rotate clockwise very slightly on the backswing, opening the blade, and on the forward swing rotate counterclockwise, closing the blade through impact. Most slicers either reverse these rotations or never rotate their hands and arms correctly in the forward swing, leaving the clubface open at impact.

To get the feeling of the "draw" action, there's nothing better than the "baseball" drill. Take a sand wedge and set up to an imaginary ball. Now stand erect, bringing the arms and club up in one piece so that the club is horizontal at chest height. As you swing the club back, and the body turns in sympathy with the swing, you'll find that the weight of the wedge forces your hands and arms to rotate the club clockwise and the right arm to fold as the wrists cock. At the "top" of the swing, the clubface faces the sky. On the forward swing, the wedge makes you rotate your

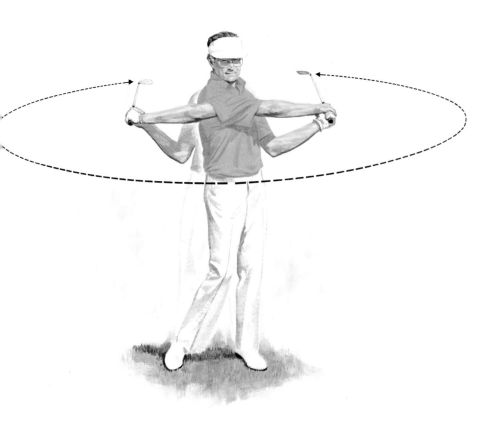

hands and arms strongly counterclockwise through "impact," and on the follow-through, the right arm straightens, the left arm folds, and the clubface finishes facedown. Perform several "baseball" swings, then hit a ball normally with, say, a 5-iron. If you overdo it and hook, don't worry. It's not difficult to reduce the amount of rotation back and through until the hook becomes a gentle draw.

If you're a confirmed slicer, work this drill into every practice session. If you suddenly start slicing, the drill will make correction a breeze.

Light Is Right

Too many golfers take a death grip on the club at address. Often this is because they don't want anything to go wrong, and feel that a tight grip will give them maximum control. In fact, too tight a grip will stiffen the forearms and wrists, preventing a proper release and killing power. Too tight a grip at address can also cause the hands to tire as the backswing progresses, and at the top of the swing, the back three fingers of the left hand will loosen and/or the palm of the right hand will come away from the left thumb. In fact, then, a tight grip leads to a *loss* of control.

Another reason golfers initially hold too tightly is because of the so-called pressure points in the grip. They have been told that at address they must grip more tightly with the back three fingers of the left hand, for example. They then take a death grip on the club, with the unpleasant results outlined above.

Instead of a tight grip, hold the club lightly but securely at address, with an even pressure in both hands. Then, as you swing back, the outward tug of the centrifugal force you create in the club will cause you to gradually increase your grip pressure at two points: in the back three fingers

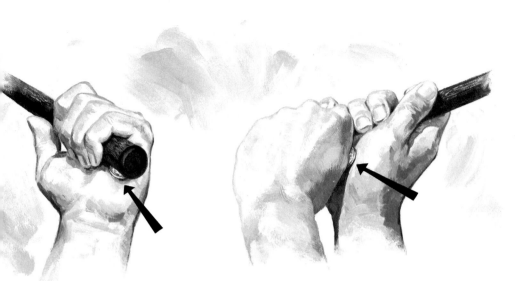

of the left hand and the palm of the right hand pressing on the left thumb.

If you've always used a light grip, this gradual increase of pressure will have become an automatic response to the centrifugal force. However, if you've always gripped too tightly, you may overdo the light grip when you first try it. That is when I'd recommend the "coin test," using two dimes or pennies. Put one coin between the heel of your left hand and the club, the other between your right palm and left thumb (see illustration). If you can keep the coins in place as you swing, your grip pressure will be just right.

Watch Your Ball Position

When most seniors have directional problems with their swing, they look first for problems in the swing itself. This is usually the wrong approach. If you're an experienced golfer, and most seniors are, the first thing you should look at is your address position, and the first thing to check at address is the position of the ball in relation to your feet. If the ball is in the wrong position, it makes you pull or push the shot. Here's how it works.

When the ball is in the normal (or correct) position in relation to the feet, about off the left heel with a driver, then your swing will approach the ball from inside the target line. You swing through the ball along the line, then back to the inside of the line (see illustrations). If the ball is too far back in the stance, you tend to close your shoulders, and as a result, you swing through the ball from inside to outside the line, pushing it to the right. The opposite is true with the ball too far forward in the stance—you tend to open your shoulders and pull the ball to the left.

If you're merely pulling or pushing the ball, moving the ball back or forward in the stance to its "normal" position will cure the problem. However, if you're also curving the ball, you'll need further help.

When you start slicing the ball, you tend to play the ball forward in an attempt to allow for the slice by aiming to the left. Now, since you've opened your shoulders, instead of the ball's starting straight and slicing, it's pulled to the left and then slices back. It's better to correct the pull first by bringing the ball back to its normal position so that it starts on line, and then cure the slice. Most slicers have too

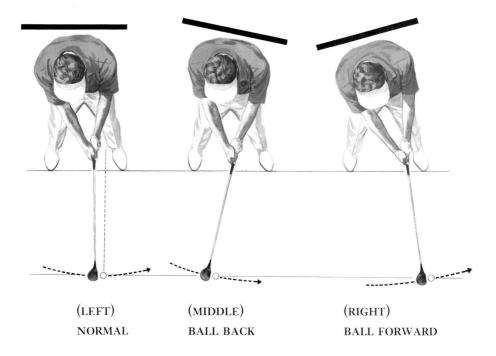

(LEFT) (MIDDLE) (RIGHT)

NORMAL BALL BACK BALL FORWARD

weak a grip, with both hands turned too much to the left on the club. At impact, the hands tend to turn to the right, opening the clubface. So, the first thing to try is a slightly stronger grip, both hands turned more to the right. If this doesn't effect a cure, work on the baseball drill (page 120).

Hookers need the opposite medicine. They tend to allow for their hook by aiming to the right and playing the ball back too far in the stance. As a result, the ball is pushed to the right, then hooks back. They should first correct the push by playing the ball more forward in its normal position, then correct the hook by adopting a weaker grip, both hands turned more to the left.

125

Fairway Bunkers—
Catch It Cleanly

When you have a good lie in a fairway bunker and want to
play a full shot with an iron, the keys to success are catch-

ing the ball first, and catching it cleanly. Hit behind the ball and the shot is ruined.

As you set up, work your feet into the sand enough so that you stabilize your body. Then, to compensate for the lower position of the feet and also for control, choke down about an inch on the club. In order to catch the ball first, play the ball back a little in the stance. If anything, keep your weight slightly on the left side. This encourages you to break your wrists earlier than usual and hit down slightly more steeply, making contact a little higher on the back of the ball than normal.

To aid the correct contact, change your point of focus on the ball. Normally, you should focus on the bottom of the ball, where you want to hit it. However, on this shot, focus higher on the back of the ball.

The swing should be very controlled, and of about three-quarter length. Think of swinging mostly with the arms and hands. You don't want a big, hard swing, with a lot of body motion and leg action, because then you're liable to slip in the sand and not strike the ball solidly. To compensate, take one stronger club than you normally would for the distance.

If you were going to play a 5-wood from a bunker, you should do most of the same things: Work your feet into the sand, choke down slightly, and take a controlled swing. However, with a 5-wood, don't put more weight on your left foot, or break the wrists quickly. Just play the ball back a little farther back than normal in your stance to help you catch the ball cleanly. With all the loft on the club, you should be able to get the ball out without having to hit down too much. The swing, therefore, would be pretty much a normal wood swing, with a wide one-piece take-away and a sweeping hit.

Downhill Lies

When your ball is on a downhill lie, the most important adjustment is to position your body so that you can swing through the ball parallel to the slope. This involves lowering your left shoulder, putting more weight on your left foot. From this position, you reduce the loft on the club and hit the ball on a lower trajectory than usual. For this reason, select a club with more loft. Even so, you may find that, in approaching a green, you must let the ball bounce short and roll on rather than attempting to carry the ball all the way onto the green. You should also play the ball back in the stance to ensure catching it cleanly and avoid the possibility of fat shots.

If you followed these instructions on more severe downhill lies, you would put too much weight on the left foot and lose your balance. In such situations, you should stand with your body more vertical and the right knee flexed more than normally.

On a downhill lie, the whole body tends to fall down the slope to the left in the downswing, and the hands and club come into the ball late, leaving the clubface open and causing a fade. So aim slightly to the left to allow for it. In fact, it's a good idea to use a slightly open stance and play for a fade—you'll find it far easier to get through the ball with an open stance than a square one. Also, in a fade swing, the club comes through the ball not only on an out to in path, but descends more steeply on the ball than on a straight shot swing. This descending angle of attack helps you get the ball up in the air.

The other important point to realize about these lies is that it's all too easy to lose your balance and mis-hit the shot. Choke down slightly for control and take a slightly

restricted swing. The steeper the downhill lie, the less you should use your body and the more you should stay centered and use your hands and arms.

Uphill Lies

When the ball is on an uphill lie, the most important adjustment is, as with downhill lies, to position the body in such a way that you can swing through parallel to the slope. To put your body more at right angles to the slope, raise your left shoulder, thus placing more weight on your right foot. Also, play the ball more forward in the stance. With such an address, you effectively increase the loft on the club, and hit the ball on a higher trajectory than normal. So, you will need a less lofted club than usual to hit the ball a specific distance.

If you tried to get your body at right angles to the slope on a severe uphill lie, you would be forced to put too much weight on your right foot, and you'd lose your balance. When you have such a lie, you must make a further adjustment—stand more vertically, and bend your left knee more than usual. Use a square stance.

In the swing, the problem is getting through the ball. Because you have more weight on the right foot than usual, it becomes more difficult on mild uphill lies—and nearly impossible on severe lies—to transfer the weight to the left foot at the start of the downswing. As a result, you'll instinctively hit the ball more with your hands and arms. As a rule, you'll release the club sooner than usual, the early rotation of the club through the ball will close the clubface at impact, and you'll pull or draw the ball to the left. To allow for this, aim a little right of the target.

As on the downhill lie, keeping your balance is the key. The more severe the lie, the more you must stay centered and hit the ball with your arms and hands. This will result in a power loss. So, while on a moderate uphill lie you might need, say, one stronger club than usual, on a severe lie you should go to two clubs stronger and swing very easily.

Irons from the Rough: Short, Steep, and Open

ADDRESS

IMPACT

This is a common trouble shot: Your ball goes into the rough and it is too severe for a wood but you want to get maximum distance with an iron. Here's how you should play the shot.

First of all, you shouldn't consider using any club less

lofted than a 5-iron. At impact, the grass tends to wrap around the hosel of the club, stopping it slightly so that the clubface closes. With a long iron, you would run the risk of never getting the ball up in the air.

Second, you must change your swing in order to put the club on the ball with a minimum of grass between the clubface and the ball. Instead of using the normal sweeping action, where you'd have to plow through a foot of grass behind the ball, change to a steeper swing with the club going up and down more abruptly. To do that, play the ball about in the center of the stance, a little back of its normal position with a middle iron. Grip more firmly with your left hand, open your stance a bit, and break your wrists more quickly than usual, taking the club up on a more upright plane. On the downswing, hit down steeply on the ball, pulling through strongly with your left hand, which will keep the clubface open.

Despite these efforts, the closing effect of the grass wrapping around the hosel through impact can still occur. That's why I recommend setting up with a slightly open blade before taking your grip. Then, if the clubface closes slightly because of the grass, it will close to no more than a square position, still giving the shot enough height to get up and out of the rough. (See the smaller illustrations.) If the grass doesn't close the blade, the shot will just fly a little higher.

In effect you're cutting the ball out of the rough, and getting the maximum height and stop possible. You can use exactly the same methods with any full iron shot from the rough. However, you'll usually find that some grass will get between the clubface and ball at impact, and you will lose backspin, so if you're hitting into a green, it's normally a good plan to allow the ball to bounce short and roll on.

133

The Soft Lob

One shot every senior should practice is the soft lob. It solves a common problem, that of short pitch shots over a hazard to a tight pin placement (see lower illustration). In this situation, my pro-am partners often try to pitch the ball with a short, fast swing, trying to get as much backspin as possible, which proves ineffective. Here's why.

Generally, the closer your ball lies to the green, the shorter the swing you must make. The shorter the swing, the less clubhead speed you'll generate, and the less backspin you can put on the ball. In other words, you're fighting reality if you try a short, brisk swing. Also, it's very easy to mis-hit the shot with a fast swing. The right way to go is exactly the opposite: *use a longer, lazier swing.*

Take your sand wedge and open the blade. Further increase the club's effective loft by playing the ball a little forward in a slightly open stance, with your hands positioned over the ball rather than ahead of it as on a normal pitch. You've now pre-programmed a high shot. To lock it in, so to speak, hold the club more firmly than usual.

The swing itself is very slow—if you think of using around half your normal swing speed, you'll get it right. Then, to compensate for the slow tempo, swing back about twice as far as you normally would for a shot of that distance, then swing through the same amount, the firm hands keeping the face of the club open (see upper illustration).

I must emphasize that there's not a lot of wrist or hand action in the shot. On the forward swing, the weight on the flange will cause the right hand to pass under the left a little bit, further kicking the ball in the air, but don't try to "help" the club do this with a flip or throw of the hands— you'll probably overdo it and "scoop" up on the ball, topping it. Just swing the club back with your arms, your shoulders going along for the ride, then swing through with your arms, allowing your right knee to ease through the shot.

You'll find that the ball will come off the club slowly, but because of the open face and increased loft, it will fly fairly high and drop dead on the green. If you have an indifferent lie, play the same shot with a pitching wedge.

The Equator Shot

One of the toughest lies is when your ball runs through the green and comes to rest on the apron, but against the collar of rough. If you try to putt the ball, either your putter catches in the rough and the ball goes nowhere, or, if you are careful to avoid the rough, you hit the ball thin, and again the ball doesn't roll in a predictable fashion. If you try to chip the ball, you're forced to deloft the club and hit down so much that you tend to hit the ball too far. Actually, this *used* to be one of the toughest lies. Now, with a technique we've found on the Tour, it actually is not too tough a shot.

Essentially, what you do is "putt" the ball *with your sand wedge*. To understand how the shot works, remember that your sand wedge has a flange with some bounce on it. In other words, the sole angles downward from the leading edge to the back. It's the flange that gives you the margin of safety on the shot, as you'll see.

Choke down on the sand wedge until you've effectively reduced the club to the length of your putter. Set up as though you were going to make a putt. Use your putting grip, putting stance, everything except ball position. You want to play the ball a little forward of normal so that you can set up with the shaft of the club inclined away from the hole (see the illustration). This brings the flange of the sand wedge into play. Address the ball with the club off the ground and the flange opposite the equator of the ball. Then go ahead and hit the equator with the flange. You'll find that, with practice, you'll be able to put a very good roll on the ball and mentally can think of the shot as though it were a putt.

I warn you: The first time you try this, it's going to appear peculiar to you, and unfamiliarity with the shot can prove fatal out on the course. The next time you're going out for some putting practice, bring your sand wedge along and hit a few equator shots of different lengths right on the practice green. Once you're used to the thought of "putting" with your sand wedge, you'll find that the shot is both fun and very effective.

LOU GRAHAM

LOU GRAHAM

Born in Nashville, Tennessee, in 1938, Lou Graham took up golf at age ten. He learned to play well enough to get a scholarship to Memphis State University, but quit school after three weeks to go into the Army. After his discharge in 1962, he worked at two Baltimore clubs before heading for the Tour in 1964. Graham was a steady performer on Tour, winning six events. His greatest moment came at the 1975 U.S. Open at Medinah. After being eleven strokes off the pace after two rounds, he shot 68 to pull himself up to four shots off the lead, then finished with 73, and a total of 287, to tie John Mahaffey. He won the playoff 71 to 73. Later in the year, he teamed with Johnny Miller to win the World Cup for the United States. His most lucrative year on Tour was 1979, when he won three events in a matter of eight weeks and finished the season with earnings of $190,827. Graham was a member of the 1973, 1975, and 1979 Ryder Cup teams. Since he joined the Senior Tour in 1988, Graham's nearest brush with victory came at the Legends of Golf where he and Tommy Aaron lost a six-hole playoff to Orville Moody and Bruce Crampton. Graham finished the year sixteenth on the money list, with earnings of $211,948.

Get the Right Hold

When I'm playing in pro-ams, the most common question I get from my amateur partners is how they can get more distance. They're looking for some sort of magic swing tip to get more of their body into the shot. Yet they've got the key right there in their own hands. So many of these golfers have some of the worst-looking grips in the world, and they don't realize that the grip is one of the most important fundamentals *for power*.

The reason is simple. The correct grip works much like the transmission of a car. When your grip is right, all the power built up by the body is transmitted through the arms and wrists to the hands and then the club. With a faulty grip, you can't control the club, and the power never gets there. We pros are always checking and rechecking our grips. You should, too.

In the left hand, the grip should run from the middle joint of the forefinger across the hand and then under the heel of the hand (illustration 1). When you close the grip, the club should be firmly pinned between the back three fingers and heel of the hand, with the left thumb positioned slightly to the right of center of the shaft (illustration 2). One of the most common errors among amateurs is to put the club too much in the palm and so fail to get enough of the heel of the hand on top of the grip for firm support. If your glove becomes worn in the heel area, then this most likely is your problem.

Here's a quick test: Take your left-hand grip, and raise the club to waist level. If the grip is correct, you should be able to take your last three fingers and thumb off the club and easily support it with just the forefinger and heel of the hand (as shown in illustration 1).

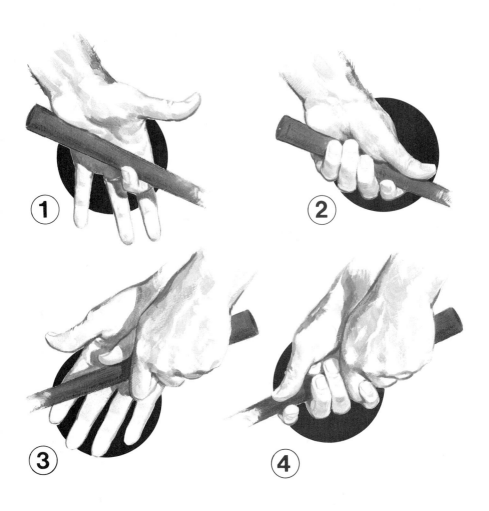

In the right hand, the key is to fit the lifeline of the right hand snugly on the left thumb (as shown in illustrations 3 and 4). Do that, and when you waggle the club, the completed grip will feel as though you have one big hand holding on the club rather than two hands. That's exactly right.

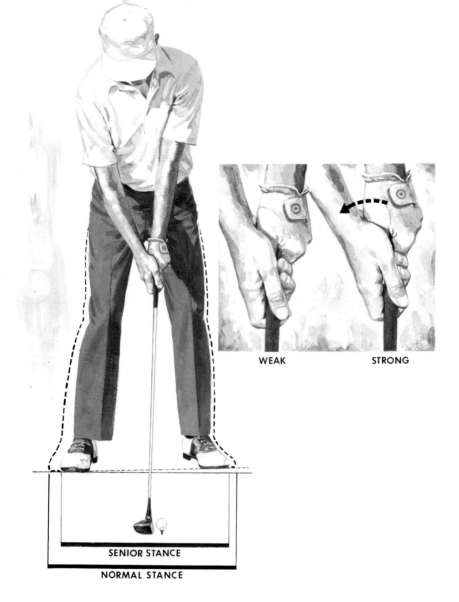

WEAK   STRONG

SENIOR STANCE

NORMAL STANCE

Seniors, It's Time for a Change of Address

As I got older, I found that a few simple adjustments to my address really helped my game. I'm sure they will help

144

you, too. The adjustments are a slightly stronger grip, a different body alignment, and a narrower stance.

When you're young, you generally have fairly strong hand action—in other words, through impact, you rotate the club strongly counterclockwise. But as you get older, you tend to lose some hand action, and with less rotation, you leave the clubface open at impact and fade or slice the ball. A fade or slice gives up too much distance compared with, say, a draw. A gentle draw is the ideal flight for seniors. To get more rotation that will square the clubface at impact or even close it slightly for a draw, change your grip. If it presently looks like the illustration labeled "weak," then turn both hands to the right before you take your grip, as in the illustration labeled "strong."

When you draw the ball, you should also modify your alignment and swing path. There are two ways to do this, and you'll have to experiment to see which suits you best. One is to set up with your feet and shoulders aligned to the right of target—on the Senior Tour, Billy Casper now uses this method. I've tried it, but it makes me hook the ball too much. If this happens to you, too, then do what I do: Set up with a slightly open stance, which helps me get through the ball, and merely swing through slightly to the right of target.

The third adjustment is in the width of your stance. As you get older, you tend to lose some leg action, and with too wide a stance you don't get back to the left side in the downswing. You start coming over the top of the ball with the right shoulder and swing through from out to in, slicing the ball. A slightly narrower stance will help you make a good weight shift to the right foot going back, and a strong return of the weight to the left foot coming through.

To Lengthen Your Backswing, Think *Hips*

If you have lost distance over the years, and your friends tell you that your backswing is not as long as it used to be, study your hip turn. When you're young, you're usually flexible enough so that if you think of turning your shoulders, your hips will turn on their own. This will no longer be true if, as a senior, you've lost some flexibility in the waist, or if you now have a lot of waist to turn.

Try this test. Stand in front of a full-length mirror, and take as full a backswing as you can. Then stop and study the image in the mirror. I'll bet that your position will closely resemble the illustration on the left. Note that the hips have hardly moved at all, even though the shoulders have turned fully and arms have swung up. One reason is given above—a lack of flexibility. A second reason is more subtle and often escapes notice. As we get older, our lower body simply doesn't work quite as well as it once did. You have to *make* it work—you can't assume it will work by itself.

Now take a second swing. This time, make a conscious effort to turn your hips as fully as you can while also turning your shoulders. Allow your left heel to be pulled from the ground if necessary. You'll be amazed at how much freer the whole backswing becomes. Your weight shift is better, your leg action is better, with the left knee breaking behind the ball, and best of all, the full hip turn has allowed you to make a longer and stronger windup as in the illustration on the right.

I should add that many seniors react to the news that their backswing has become noticeably shorter by lengthening it in the wrong way—by bending their left arm ex-

146

cessively or even letting go of the club with their hands. Such methods may lead to an occasional longer shot, but as a rule they don't work and you won't strike the ball solidly.

I hope I have convinced you that the right way to tackle the problem is to concentrate on the hip turn. As you make your takeaway, feel as though you're taking the club back with your hip turn. As you've seen, this will give you a stronger backswing, and you should see a healthy increase in distance.

Even better, your friends will no longer be talking about how short your backswing has become!

Dig It Out

Most seniors I've played with seem to be really afraid of buried lies in a bunker. They're not exactly my favorite shots, either! However, I assure you if you use the right technique, you will get the ball out every time. Although there are basically two types of buried lie—the regular buried lie, and the "fried egg" lie, where the ball is sitting in a crater of sand—the same method will handle both.

First, you should understand that the technique for a buried lie is different from that used for a regular trap shot. From a good lie, you want the sand wedge to skid through, taking a shallow cut, so you open the blade to bring the bounce on the flange into play. But to extricate the ball from a buried lie, the wedge must dig down deeply beneath the ball so that the ball comes out with the displaced sand. To make the sand wedge dig, you must square the blade, as shown in the two smaller illustrations.

Set up with the ball back in a slightly open stance, and put more weight on your left foot. These two adjustments set up the steeply descending blow you need. The swing itself should be mostly a hands, arms, and shoulders effort, with very little leg work. Break the wrists quickly off the ball, taking the club up sharply. Then hit down steeply between two and three inches behind the ball. Don't hit closer to the ball than this—a common mistake—as you may not be able to hit down and under it. In the down-swing, also be careful not to move your weight too quickly to the left side; in that case, you'll tend to dig too deeply and never get the club through the ball. Use only enough leg work in the downswing to control your balance. Your follow-through on this shot will be shorter than usual, which is due to the resistance of the sand, but you should still try to hit through the ball as much as possible—the club must cut down under the ball and continue through for you to get it out. Because of the amount of sand you excavate behind the ball, you can't put spin on this shot, and must allow for a fair amount of run.

A Tough Lie

When your ball lies in the bunker, but you're forced to take your stance on the ground outside it, the most important adjustment is to get your hands and the club down to ball level in the correct way.

Although the amount of adjustment depends on how far below your feet the ball lies, you will always have to take a wider stance than normal, flex your knees more than usual, and lean over more than for a regular shot. In leaning forward more, make certain that you do it from the hips, as shown. If you merely lean forward from the waist, you'll be forced to make an unnatural and far steeper swing than usual, and it probably will spoil the shot. Also, you can keep the amount of adjustment to a minimum by gripping the club at the end of the grip. This is one shot on which you should not choke down.

This is an extreme example of a ball-below-feet lie, so you must expect to push the ball off to the right. The lower the ball is, the farther left of target you must aim. Otherwise, set up as you would on a normal explosion shot, with a slightly open stance and blade, and plan to enter the sand about one and a half inches behind the ball.

There are two common problems that seniors seem to have with this shot. The first is not staying down to the shot. Because your legs are bent more than usual, the tendency is to come out of your knee flex and thin or even top the ball. Make an extra effort to retain your knee flex from address until well after impact. The second problem is caused by your standing outside the bunker on firm ground. It feels like you're hitting the ball from the ground rather than from sand, so you don't allow for the resistance of the sand and you underhit the shot. A contributing fac-

tor is that you don't really know how soft the sand is. At any rate, force yourself to hit the shot with a force that *feels* much firmer than usual, and you'll actually swing with the right amount of strength.

Let 'em Laugh: Putt from the Sand

Although I very rarely putt from a bunker, it sometimes can be the best percentage shot. However, I should emphasize that all the conditions have to be right for the putter shot to work. If just one of the conditions is wrong, it's far safer to play a normal explosion.

Obviously, the first requirement is that the ball must lie cleanly on the sand. Forget about using the putter if the ball is even slightly buried. Secondly, if the sand is soft or if it's all churned up, the ball won't roll smoothly and it becomes too difficult to judge the strength of the shot. The sand should be very firm and the surface very smooth all the way up to the lip. The lip itself must be low, and the grass on the lip should be closely mowed—a high lip or a lot of shaggy grass on the lip tells you to keep the putter in the bag.

Assuming everything else is right, two factors can almost force you to use a putter. If the ball is on a downhill lie—especially a severe downhill lie—where it is very difficult to make an explosion shot and get the ball to sit down on the green and where you also run the risk of thinning or blading the ball over the green, definitely take your putter. Or if you don't have much green to work with, making an explosion shot "iffy," then again take the putter.

As for the stroke itself, just make your normal putter stroke. Remember, of course, that you can't ground your

YES

NO

putter behind the ball. I saw a player who will be nameless do that one time and have to take a two-stroke penalty! Apparently, because he had a putter in his hand and was concentrating so hard, he simply forgot where he was. Since the sand will provide more resistance than grass, you must hit the putter shot from sand harder than a normal putt of the same length. However, I can't give you an exact rule on this like, say, hit it twice as hard. The best advice I can give you is simply to practice the shot occasionally so you develop some feel for it.

Up and Out of the Water

The first rule about playing "water shots" is not to do it unless it's strictly necessary! I've seen too many such shots fail, even when hit by the best of golfers. When a ball lies in water in a water hazard, the shot is chancy at best. But if you're in a tight situation in a match and must consider the shot, here are the points to look for.

YES   NO

As a general rule, you should only think of exploding the ball from water if your ball lies very close to the green. Water offers tremendous resistance, and you have to be extremely strong to try longer shots. Also, how the ball lies in the water is very important. If it is completely submerged, don't attempt the shot! When the ball is below the surface of the water, you never can be sure how deep it actually is—it can appear to be just below the surface, yet be, say, one inch below. Water bends light, and the ball may not be lying exactly where you think it is. You've been warned!

To play the shot, take your sand wedge—its extra weight is invaluable—and set the blade in a square position so that it will cut down into the water. Whatever you do, don't set it open—it would merely bounce off the water and into the ball. Play the ball forward in the stance—a couple of inches inside the left heel is about right—and try to enter the water about an inch behind the ball. Then you can dig down well underneath it, the most important point. The swing is pretty much the same as the one you'd use from the fairway except that you're going to have to hit the ball extremely hard!

The resistance of the water becomes critical the farther you are from the green. If I were considering a longer shot, I would never attempt it if less than half of the ball showed above the water.

Explode from Deep Rough

Many seniors I play with seem to have a lot of trouble with short pitches from heavy rough around the green. Typically, they try to hit the ball first, which means they have to hit it very easily. Since there's not enough clubhead speed, the club often gets caught up in the grass, and the result is an ineffective, even fluffed, shot. There is a better way—play the shot almost exactly as you would an explosion shot from a good lie in a bunker.

In other words, select your sand wedge and set up with a slightly open blade so that the bounce on the wedge will let it ride through the heavy grass. Hover the club behind the ball so the grass won't snag it in the takeaway. To compensate for the open blade, open your stance and shoulder alignment so that you pre-program a swing from out to in across the ball. Hold the club very firmly so that the grass doesn't twist it in your hands. In the takeaway, break your wrists more quickly than usual, taking the club outside and up. On the forward swing, instead of trying to catch the ball cleanly, aim to enter the grass about an inch behind it. Because of the resistance from the grass, you'll find that you can hit the ball more firmly than when attempting a clean hit. In fact, if you have difficulty with the strength on this shot, imagine that you actually are playing a bunker shot, and immediately you'll have a good idea of how hard to hit it.

Hit down and through the ball, but hit it with a "popping" action. Instead of swinging all the way through to a full finish, which will make the ball go too far, cut off the finish, with the club coming to a halt three or four feet after impact. You must keep the clubface open through impact; aim to finish with the clubface looking straight up.

When you play the shot correctly, you'll find the ball "pops" up from the grass very quickly and lands softly on the green. Because of all the grass that gets between the clubface and ball, you can't put much backspin on the ball, so allow for a little run.

157

Chipping Made Simple

The most important point in chipping is to keep things simple. Many seniors tie themselves up in knots over chip shots, and I have to conclude that most of you would do a lot better if you thought of the chip shot in terms of something you're familiar with, such as throwing a ball underhand.

If you were going to toss a ball to the hole, you'd turn your body to the target so as to get a good sight of it, then

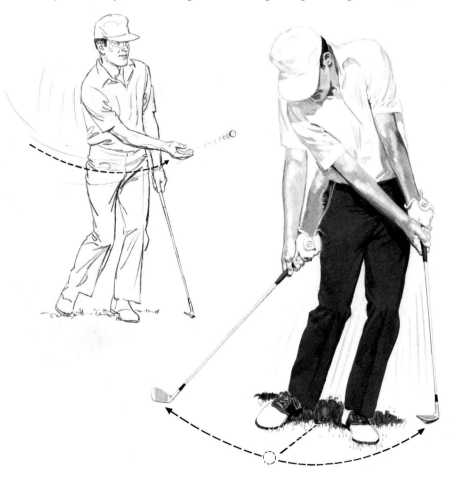

158

swing your right arm back and through with no wrist—a very simple, uncomplicated action. As much as possible, do the same in chipping. Take a very open, narrow stance, and then gauge the distance by how far you swing your right arm back and through. As in tossing the ball, it's a good idea to keep it simple and use no wrist action. In golf, this translates into using an arm-and-shoulder stroke as most Tour pros do in putting. In other words, swing your arms back and through and let your shoulders move in sympathy with the swing. However, you must bear in mind that on a wristless stroke, the shoulder line will pre-program your swing path. So to hit the ball straight, set up with your shoulders square to your intended line.

Another important point in chipping is that you must keep your hands leading the club all the way through. If the clubhead ever gets ahead of your hands, the low point of the swing arc will be behind the ball and you'll blade it or hit it fat. So put your weight well forward on your left heel and play the ball back in the center of the stance with your hands ahead of the ball. Then, if you keep your hands and wrists firm and just swing your arms, you'll hit down on the ball and avoid this problem.

If you were tossing the ball, you'd soon find that releasing it low and then letting it roll most of the way to the pin is far easier to judge and more dependable than if you lobbed it high to land close to the hole. Do the same thing in chipping. It's far easier to hit a lower-lofted club solidly than a high-lofted one, and a mis-hit with the former will always give you a better result than one with the latter. The golden rule in chipping is this: Always take the lowest-lofted club that will land the ball three feet onto the green (for a dependable bounce) and have it roll up and stop by the hole.